"I highly recommend this book to any instructor who appreciates the fact that a full understanding of American history is key to a just society. Each year, hundreds of University of Texas at Austin students take a history class with the award-winning professor Leonard Moore, and they find the class to be a life-changing experience. How does Moore reach both Black and non-Black students, and why do they go on to recommend his courses to their friends? In this book, Moore combines stories from his own life with social commentary and discussions of his teaching techniques, honed over two decades in the classroom. He begins the book with this simple observation: *Every white person in America should be required to take a Black history class in either high school or college. Period.* Moore's straightforward, no-holds-barred approach—about African American history, about the realities of race in America today—inspires students even as it enlightens them. This practical guide will prove useful for all teachers who want to educate students of all backgrounds and any age in an inclusive, compelling way. A course in Black history, taught with sensitivity and honesty by a knowledgeable instructor, as Moore illustrates here, can generate difficult but necessary conversations that are truly transformative for instructor and student alike."

—JACQUELINE JONES, UNIVERSITY OF TEXAS AT AUSTIN, AUTHOR OF *A DREADFUL DECEIT: THE MYTH OF RACE FROM THE COLONIAL ERA TO OBAMA'S AMERICA*

"*Teaching Black History to White People* is essential for any institution seeking to create or enhance an inclusive environment. Whether Dr. Moore's message is applied to the workplace or to one's personal life, its authenticity and intent won't be missed by anyone. Why? Because Black History Matters."

—SEVETRI WILSON, FOUNDER AND CEO OF RESILIA

"*Teaching Black History to White People* is a blast of fresh thought in stale conversations about race. Moore's sharp, direct style reframes old dialogues and slices to the heart of difficult challenges. Sometimes this book made me laugh out loud; other times I was encouraged by Moore's accomplishments or angered by how he has been treated. For anyone seeking to break down resistance to the true history of our nation, this book is an absolute gem."

—JESSE WASHINGTON, SENIOR WRITER AT ESPN.COM'S *THE UNDEFEATED* AND COAUTHOR OF *I CAME AS A SHADOW*, THE AUTOBIOGRAPHY OF JOHN THOMPSON

"I watched Dr. Leonard Moore masterfully teach Black history when he was my professor at Louisiana State University. As a young, Black college student, I was inspired by his boldness, passion, and commitment to speaking truth to power. His teaching methods provided a platform that encouraged meaningful dialogue and critical thinking. Everyone grew wiser and more equipped to appreciate Black history as a result."

—DAVID "DEE-1" AUGUSTINE, FORMER STUDENT, RAPPER AND SOCIAL ACTIVIST

"If you care about the future of race relations in the United States, you need to read this book. Dr. Moore provides a valuable starting point for anyone interested in learning more about the Black experience. He is also a gifted author who weaves his personal story into the larger context of American history to help cement his key point: you cannot understand the perspective of Black people in this country without learning their history, most of which has been left untold in our classrooms."

—JOE KARLGAARD, DIRECTOR OF ATHLETICS, RICE UNIVERSITY

"I am a white male who has worked in the advertising industry for most of my career. Like those in other industries, we are beginning to understand the ways in which the complexity of white supremacy and unconscious bias affects how we work. Within this context, I believe Dr. Leonard Moore's book is both seminal and mandatory reading for starting a discourse on understanding the Black experience in our country. I will never truly know what it means to grow up Black in America nor what it means to work as a Black person in America, but Dr. Moore provides the insight to better see, feel, understand, and comprehend this truth—a truth we all must seek to understand if we are to progress as a people."

—AL REID, MARKETING DIRECTOR,
SAATCHI & SAATCHI, DALLAS

TEACHING BLACK HISTORY TO WHITE PEOPLE

TEACHING
BLACK
HISTORY TO
WHITE
PEOPLE

LEONARD N. MOORE

UNIVERSITY OF TEXAS PRESS ⬆ AUSTIN

Requests for permission to reproduce material from
this work should be sent to:
    Permissions
    University of Texas Press
    P.O. Box 7819
    Austin, TX 78713-7819
    utpress.utexas.edu/rp-form

♾ The paper used in this book meets the minimum
requirements of ANSI/NISO Z39.48-1992 (R1997)
(Permanence of Paper).

LIBRARY OF CONGRESS CATALOGING-IN-
PUBLICATION DATA

Names: Moore, Leonard N., 1971- author.
Title: Teaching Black history to white people /
    Leonard N. Moore.
Description: First edition. | Austin : University of
    Texas Press, 2021. | Includes index.
Identifiers: LCCN 2021021103
    ISBN 978-1-4773-2501-8 (cloth)
    ISBN 978-1-4773-2485-1 (paperback)
    ISBN 978-1-4773-2486-8 (ebook other)
    ISBN 978-1-4773-2487-5 (ebook)
Subjects: LCSH: Moore, Leonard N., 1971- | African
    Americans—History—Study and teaching
    (Higher)—United States. | African Americans—
    History—Study and teaching (Higher)—United
    States—Anecdotes. | Racism—History—Study
    and teaching (Higher)—United States. | African
    Americans—United States—History. | Whites—
    Education (Higher)—United States.
Classification: LCC E184.7 .M65 2021 |
    DDC 973/.0496073—dc23
LC record available at https://lccn.loc.gov/2021021103

doi:10.7560/324851

This book is dedicated to the memory of Ezekiel and Bessie Moore, and to the memory of Myrtis and Ada Burton.

CONTENTS

INTRODUCTION xiii

TEACHING WHITE STUDENTS ABOUT BLACKNESS 1
TEACHING MYSELF 17
TEACHING BLACK ANGER 29
TEACHING ENSLAVEMENT AND EMANCIPATION 39
TEACHING JIM CROW 55
TEACHING BLACK URBANIZATION 77
TEACHING THE CIVIL RIGHTS MOVEMENT 95
TEACHING BLACK POWER 120
TEACHING WHITE LIBERALS 148

CONCLUSION 161

ACKNOWLEDGMENTS 165
APPENDIX: Syllabus for History of the Black Experience 166
SUGGESTED READING 170
INDEX 178

INTRODUCTION

EVERY WHITE PERSON IN AMERICA SHOULD BE required to take a Black history class in either high school or college. Period. Although this may seem like a radical statement, it is actually rooted in reason and practicality. White Americans have been allowed to avoid learning about the Black experience, and as a result many of them view Black people through a distinct stereotypical lens. Based upon my twenty-five years teaching Black history to white people, I believe that a proper understanding of our struggle is key for racial reparations, racial healing, and racial reconciliation. I've taught more than twenty thousand students, and more than half have been white. At the end of every semester the reviews from white students often read like this: "Dr. Moore, thank you for changing my life. I was ignorant about the struggles of Black people but now I get it. I can't believe I didn't learn any of this stuff in middle school or high school." During the semester white students will often wait for me after class to talk about how the class has impacted them and how they now see the world differently. I've witnessed borderline racists, like one student you will read about later, have a complete change of heart over the course of fifteen weeks. Even parents, university staff, and alumni who sit in on my classes have been transformed.

Teaching in the Deep South for two decades has convinced me that white students and their families are secretly craving to learn more about Black History, and they are not afraid to be intellectually challenged. Black history is not a "difficult subject"; it is an amazing and empowering subject. While I initially went to Louisiana State University to teach Black history as a tool for motivating Black students, it has been impactful for white students as well. If you were to poll all of the white students who've taken my classes over the years, I am sure a large majority of them would say that of the classes they've taken, mine had and continues to have the biggest impact on their lives. This is not meant to be boastful or arrogant but is simply the truth. Imagine getting to college and never being exposed to any aspect of Black history. When white students take my class they become a sponge, and it convinces many of them that they have been lied to by their communities, their families, and their school systems.

Some of my friends and family members say that it isn't *our* (Black folks') responsibility to teach *them* (white people) our history—they need to learn it on their own. While I understand this sentiment, I disagree. If we don't teach it to them, who will? If you look at some of the absurd controversies surrounding the teaching of Black history in the K–12 setting, it becomes clear that the college classroom is the best place to teach it. If we are ever going to have open and honest conversations about the country's racial past, then that conversation starts and ends with the teaching and learning of Black history.

This is an unusual book. It is part memoir, part Black history, part pedagogy, and part how-to guide. The project is largely based upon a series of virtual lectures on the Black experience that I delivered during the racially tumultuous summer of 2020 to an audience that was probably 80 percent white. Speaking to a large white audience about Black history was not new to me. I've been doing it for more than twenty years at both Louisiana State University and the University of Texas at Austin, two schools located in the heart of the former Confederacy, in two states that have a brutal legacy of racial oppression. The first part of the book chronicles many of these unique experiences both inside the classroom and out, and it attempts to explain how an understanding of Black history is critical to racial reconciliation and healing.

The second part of the book is a narrative arc of Black history from the colonial period through the 1970s. This is not a comprehensive examination of the Black experience but a highlight of the key periods, ideas, and movements that help explain contemporary Black America. As I got deeper into the book project, I decided to connect my lived experiences and those of my extended family to those of the larger African American community. My father's family migrated from Indianapolis to Cleveland in 1945 before settling in Los Angeles in 1961. My mother's family never left rural Franklinton, Louisiana. So I grew up with a mother who was reared in a vibrant, self-sustaining, all-Black rural Southern community but whose childhood was impacted by segregation, disenfranchisement, racial intimidation, and the horrific lynching of her cousin, Jerome Wilson, in 1935. My dad never lived in the South, and he'd had no intention of ever visiting the South until he met my mom in 1957. He and his side of the family lived through the Second Great Migration and the resulting challenges of ghettoization, redlining and housing discrimination, poor schooling, police brutality, and labor union discrimination and racist hiring practices. The experiences of the Moores and the Burtons typify much of the Black experience in twentieth-century America, and at times I share those stories in this book.

The last chapter, "Teaching White Liberals," provides a guideline on what well-meaning white people can do to ease the tension over race in America. During the summer of 2020 I was flooded with emails, texts, and phone calls from colleagues and friends who sincerely wanted to know what they could do. This chapter answers that question.

You will notice that unlike traditional history books, this project does not have any footnotes or references. That is intentional. I tried to write this book the way I teach, with humor, provocation, anecdotes, and stories. I have found this approach to be helpful when teaching Black history to white people.

TEACHING BLACK HISTORY TO WHITE PEOPLE

TEACHING WHITE STUDENTS ABOUT BLACKNESS

NOVEMBER 25, 2014, WAS ONE OF THE MOST MEMorable days I have had in my twenty-three years as a professor. The night before, the St. Louis County district attorney decided not to indict Ferguson police officer Darren Wilson in the shooting death of Michael Brown. That evening my family and I watched the CNN coverage of the Ferguson protest for several hours. While the commentators focused on the violence, the looting, and the lack of civil order, my wife and I talked about the long pattern of police brutality in America and why Ferguson's residents reacted angrily.

When I went to sleep that night, I knew my Black Power class would be filled not only with my students but with students not enrolled in the class, alumni, and interested staff. Generally speaking, white students wanted to know why Black people would burn down their communities. Black students wanted to know how a white police officer could get away with killing an unarmed Black man in 2014. I tried to write down some thoughts that night, but I couldn't come up with anything.

When I got to the office that morning, one of my grad students said, "Doc, I'm coming to class today. . . . I gotta hear this." As the clock approached eleven I put on my suit jacket and walked across Dean Keeton Street to Burdine Hall. I had no idea what I was going to say. When I walked onstage the class was full, with people sitting in the aisles and some standing outside the classroom double doors. I put on the microphone and pulled a chair to the front of the stage and said the following: "I know what all of you want to talk about and I'm gonna let you talk to each other. Remember, you can't get mad and we will be tolerant and respectful of opinions we disagree with."

For the next seventy-five minutes, students of all races stood up and expressed their opinions on Ferguson and the rest of us listened. Afterward, students expressed appreciation for me letting them talk, although some had come expecting me to preach about Ferguson. As I left class that day, I saw students standing outside Burdine Hall continuing the discussion in productive ways.

ON THE FIRST DAY OF CLASS EVERY FALL SEMESTER I walk from my office and head to the large lecture room in the University Teaching Center. It holds more than five hundred seats. As I walk in the first time, the room is buzzing with excitement, anticipation, and energy. It's packed, with some students even sitting on the steps at the front of the room. I guess they want to get a good seat. When I look out at all 550 students, I see how racially diverse the class is. Black students congregate in the middle center; football players sit in the first few rows; Nigerian Americans in the front left; Latinos in the front center; white liberals in the middle left; feminists up near the front; and in the back left is a large contingent of white fraternity members.

They are noticeable because of their distinct look—they proudly wear their Greek T-shirts as a status symbol.

To find so many white frat members in my class, History of the Black Power Movement, is shocking. When I first started teaching the course during my second year on the University of Texas faculty in the fall of 2008, the class was approximately 80 percent African American, with a total enrollment of 150 to 200 students. It was so Black that we called the experience a miniature HBCU (historically Black college or university). But over time, as the class has become larger and more popular, it has become increasingly white.

When many white students walk into my course, they experience a series of firsts: The first time many of them have had a Black teacher or professor. The first time many of them have ever taken a class dealing with African American history. The first time many of them have been in a class with so many Black and Latino students. The first time many of them have taken a class that does not meet their parents' approval. The first time many of them have felt like a minority. The first time many of them will be in a class that forces them to confront their whiteness.

The white Greek presence in the class is interesting because this population is typically the most conservative, the most privileged, and the one that unfortunately throws racially themed frat parties in West Campus. In no way am I suggesting that these students are racist, just that they have been shielded from any discussion about the Black experience in America. For a country that has been shaped by race, we do young people a disservice when we allow them to go through their K–12 years without a Black history course because we are afraid to confront the brutal realities of race in America.

"Welcome to History of the Black Power Movement," I say at the beginning of the first class. "This is HIS 317L . . . so make sure you are in the right place. To be clear, this is a class about Black people, from a Black perspective, and taught by a Black professor. White students? Are we clear about that? This is not a Black history class taught from your perspective—this is not Black history on white people's terms. You are here because you really want to understand the Black experience. The reason I am explicit about how the class will be taught is because on a teaching evaluation several years ago, one student wrote that she didn't enjoy the class because it was too focused on Black people!"

I continue: "As you see, I am not politically correct and don't plan to be. We are overly sensitive about race in this country, and this prevents us from having an open, honest dialogue. Please understand we will deal with sensitive issues in this class that most professors will not deal with. But I have some ground rules.

"Rule No. 1: You can say whatever you want in this class. Rule No. 2: You cannot get mad at another student's comment. Rule No. 3: There are no stupid questions. We are here to learn. Rule No. 4: I am very opinionated, but you don't have to agree with me to do well in the class. Rule No. 5: I am not here to change the way you think. I just want you to look at the Black experience through a Black lens. Rule No. 6: We will have fun and create a bond over the next fifteen weeks. Rule No. 7: You will remember this class thirty years from now. Rule No. 8: You will always refer to me as 'the Black professor I had at UT.'" They always laugh at number eight because many of them don't know me as Dr. Moore or Professor Moore. They know me as "the Black guy who teaches the Black history class."

The end of the first day of class is always interesting because I typically have a bunch of students who want to speak to me after class. Some of the comments I get are as follows:

- "My friend told me to take this class, and I know I am going to like it."
- "I'm a business major, and I've never had a class like this. I grew up in a very conservative environment, so a lot of this will be new to me."
- "I just want you to know that I probably won't agree with everything you say."
- "I know I look like the typical white guy, but I have a ton of Black friends."
- "This class will be good for me because I don't know much about Black history, although I dated a Black guy in high school."
- "I've started to read the assigned books and this is fascinating."

I typically assign five required books for the class, including *Negroes with Guns* by Robert F. Williams and *Die Nigger Die!* by H. Rap Brown. I have been told it is an instant conversation piece with their friends and roommates when many of my white students purchase *Negroes with Guns* and *Die Nigger Die!* I ask about this phenomenon in class, and they speak about the questions they are asked:

- "What are you taking that class for? Is it required?"
- "Why does this class exist?"
- "Are there any other white students in the class?"
- "What does it feel like in there?"

And my all-time favorite:

- "Does the professor hate white people?"

Additionally, some white students have mentioned the responses they get from their parents when they tell them about the class:

- "Now, don't get up to Austin and become a liberal."
- "Why would UT offer a class like that?"
- "I hope the class doesn't teach you that we are to blame for all of their problems; slavery ended a long time ago."

There are always several white students who say that they discuss the course lectures with their parents every Tuesday and Thursday evening over the phone. In fact, one set of parents got a copy of the syllabus and read the books along with their daughter who was enrolled in the course. One of these same parents sent me a thank you letter at the end of one semester for helping her and her daughter get another perspective on the Black experience. Although the mom admitted she hadn't wanted her daughter to take the course, she realized that it helped both of them grow in amazing ways.

The class is in lecture format, but I do my best to make it interactive, interesting, and engaging. I typically start class by posing a provocative question to the students, such as: "Can white teachers effectively teach Black children?" "What came first, slavery or racism?" "Has integration failed Black people?"

Then we are off and running. I want to make the class as interactive as possible, because in an era where Google has the content, the role of the professor is to facilitate, engage, inspire, and prepare them for the real world. And ironically, with 550 students, the class becomes like a town hall meeting.

There are several lectures during the semester where it seems like white students begin to understand. The first occurs on the second day, when I show graphic images of African Americans being lynched. In all of the images there is usually a group of whites surrounding the victim, smiling and posing for photographs. When I put up the first image the class becomes eerily silent. Some students stare at the image while others put their head down. Then I ask the question, what could this person have done to deserve this? Why are the people standing next to the corpse smiling? Why do the people appear to be well dressed? Why are there kids in the photo? If you were a white kid and you witnessed this, how would this affect you for the rest of your life? If you were Black, how would this affect you?

Another transformative moment in the class comes when we discuss the reparations movement in America. After establishing that Jim Crow was state-sanctioned discrimination, I then make a relevant application. "Since Black people in Texas could not vote until the mid-1960s, that means white voters had a one-hundred-year head start on Black voters. To address this miscarriage of justice, would it be fair to pass a law stating that white voters could not vote again until 2075?" They all say no, even the Black students. "What about all of the advantages this gave the white community?" They still say no.

When we discuss affirmative action and race in university admissions, it really touches a nerve with many students. Someone typically tells the class, "My friend, who is white, got a 1530 on his SATs, but because he wasn't top

10 percent he didn't get into UT. He went to a competitive high school, so why should someone from an inner-city school get in before him with lower test scores?" Good point. The response: "The Top 10 Percent Law rewards those who were the best in their peer group and those from similar backgrounds. So while your friend did get a 1530, he wasn't among the best in his peer group." This typically transitions us into discussions about standardized testing and whether or not these exams are measures of intelligence or are culturally biased against Black people. I help the students process this question by giving them my eight-question IQ test. I ask them to answer the following questions:

- If I told you I had to put some money on my uncle's books, what would I be talking about?
- What are Js?
- My friend spent his entire paycheck on some 22s. What does this mean?
- If you are up big in a dice game, at what point can you leave?
- What does the acronym HBCU mean?
- My grandmother recently told me that my grandfather had sugar. What is she talking about?
- Who is Thomas Dexter Jakes?
- If someone tells you that the wake starts at 5:00 p.m., what are they talking about?

Then we discuss the answers. Typically, most of the Black students get at least seven of the answers correct, while the white students get the majority of them wrong. "Now," I ask, "does that make you dumb or unqualified for college because you failed to answer these questions correctly?"

No, it just means that the questions weren't relevant to your environment.

One particular semester, several of my students in the class were members of a white fraternity that had been responsible for throwing a racially themed party in West Campus. Partygoers could swim from one side of the party to another as if they were swimming across the US-Mexico border into the United States. This, along with other racial stereotyping at the party, upset many students on campus.

When it was brought to my attention that my students were in the fraternity that held the party, I met one of the Greek students in my office. I asked him if he understood why people were mad. His response: "Dr. Moore, none of us are racist, we were just trying to have some fun." Although this was an outrageous act of racism, he could not understand why people responded angrily. He then suggested I come by his frat house to have dinner with him and his fraternity brothers. When the appointed time came for the dinner, he told me we needed to postpone it. I'm still waiting. I think he was ready to have an open discussion about race in America, but his fraternity brothers weren't.

Every semester I look forward to the first assignment. I ask the students to write a paper on how the Black experience has shaped them. You can imagine that the non-Black people in the class always have a ton of questions once the assignment is announced. "But I'm not Black, so how do I complete this paper?" said one student, who was probably asking the question on behalf of all the other non-Black students. So I then explain that although you may not be Black, the Black experience has shaped you in many ways. After a ten-minute discussion further clarifying the assignment, I tell them to turn the paper in during the next class session.

Although I have six teaching assistants for the course, I read all five hundred papers simply because it is fascinating and also because I know that people are more willing to express themselves on paper. Not only are the papers from white students revealing, but the papers from some Black students themselves reveal a sense of shame in being Black and difficulty with appreciating one's Blackness. This is the collateral damage Black people confront when they don't know their own history. Here are some of the more memorable things both white and Black students have expressed over the past few years:

EXCERPTS FROM WHITE STUDENTS' ESSAYS

- "My dad is a sixth-generation cotton farmer. . . . I distinctly remember him pressuring me to use a racial slur."
- "I had a Black friend but I could not go to his house and he could not go to my great-grandparents' house because of their language toward Black people."
- "At my father's business my father would continually catch them [Black people] sleeping, fighting, drinking, and even smoking marijuana. This is not a stereotype, this is a fact."
- "I grew up in a white suburban bubble."
- "I grew up like other middle-class white kids. . . . I had a live-in nanny."
- "I saw my Black friend get treated differently because she was Black."
- "I was accused of having 'jungle fever' because I went to prom with a Black guy."

- "My part of the neighborhood was considered the ghetto by some kids at school because my street contained not one but two houses with Black children in them."
- "I was taking a bite of my pizza when my three-year-old sister comes crying to me and says there is a monster on the slide. I begin to wonder what 'monster' can possibly be in the children's area. She grabs me by the hand and points to an African American boy who is simply smiling."
- "I was partially raised by my best friend and second mother named Ella. She is a Black woman and cares for me like I am her own son, and I love her like a mother."
- "My teachers said, 'Slavery is a thing of the past.'"
- "I went to an all-Jewish reform school."
- "Growing up as a Jew in Little Rock . . ."
- "My sister was adopted from China and I saw her deal with racism."
- "I was raised in a white Christian suburb."
- "I believed that Black kids were better than me at sports."
- "My father was a pastor but both he and my grand-father were racist."
- "To be honest, I am still uncomfortable around African Americans."
- "I am aware that as a white man I have unfair advantages."
- "In high school I saw blatant racism and discrimination against African American students."
- "Hip-hop music taught me about the Black experience."
- "I dated a Black man in college for a semester."
- "We had a Black nanny and a Black maid who lived with us."

- "As a white kid who graduated from a private school in Dallas, Texas, I have been exposed to about as much privilege as a person can ask for."
- "I grew up in Section 8 but I went to a school in an upper-class white neighborhood."
- "My dad is a police officer and he would often brag about how many 'niggers' he arrested that day."

EXCERPTS FROM BLACK STUDENTS' ESSAYS

- "I had full lips and I was happy. I took pride in a physical trait that Black people are mocked for."
- "I didn't feel the joy, power, or respect of being Black. The worse part was being degraded by my own race."
- "I was called both 'Ghetto' and 'Oreo.'"
- "Seeing other Black women wear their hair natural has inspired me to do the same."
- "'You don't sound like you're Black, you sound like a white girl.'"
- "Because society taught us that people with lighter skin were superior, we craved to act like them, to dress like them, and to speak like them."
- "Black kids called me 'Kunta Kinte' and 'African Booty Scratcher.'"
- "I learned to be Black from my white friends."
- "I was considered 'not Black' and that I was 'acting white.'"
- "As a light-skin Black I was seen as better than a dark-skin Black."
- "I would put on a ton of makeup to hide my wide nose."
- "I was the only Black student in a ton of my AP classes."
- "It was always assumed that I grew up in a broken home without a father."

- "I was called an 'oreo,' because people made fun of the way I dressed because I always tucked my shirt in, I always wore a belt, and I was kept very clean."
- "'You're pretty for a dark girl.'"
- "The Black Woman is the most unloved person in America."
- "They tried to talk me out of taking AP courses."
- "My light-skinned stepmom said I had 'soup cooler' lips."
- "I became so caught up with trying to fit in with the people around me that I didn't appreciate and embrace my Blackness."
- "The town loved me and the few Black athletes that were on the team, but once football season was done they looked at us as outsiders and treated us differently."
- "Sports has taken me to places I would have never been able to see and given me opportunities I would have never been able to have while being Black."
- "'Oh, so you're one of the smart ones.'"
- "I found out that my next-door neighbor was a high-ranking member of the KKK, yet he interacted with my family as if everything was peachy."
- "The media doesn't show Black success."
- "My Nigerian mom told me that African Americans were no good and that most of them were either not in school or in jail."
- "I was told by my science teacher that I would not be successful in life."

Although teaching white students about race, and in particular African American history, poses a unique set of challenges, many people are surprised when I tell them that teaching Black students their own history has its own unique set of challenges, as is evident from the preceding quotes. For the most part, African American students enjoy taking my class and other courses that look at the Black experience. For some, it is the only class they will take at the University of Texas where they will be surrounded by other students of color en masse. "Doc, I look forward to this class because in all of my other classes there are just two or three of us and we have to speak for the entire race." So out of a class of 550 students, roughly half will be African American, which represents about 15 percent of the university's entire Black student population.

When I first arrived at the University of Texas in the fall of 2007, I spent several days before the beginning of the semester passing out flyers about my class to Black students. For the most part they were excited and receptive. "I will definitely sign up for the class," was how most of them responded. But I did find some resistance. One African American male student told me, "I'm not gonna take the class because I'm not into that Black shit." When I asked why he wasn't interested, he gave the following rationale: "Doc, taking Black history is a waste of my time. I was born Black and I know what it is to be Black. How is this gonna help me in life? I don't see why any Black student would take a Black studies course." After probing a bit further, I learned that he was a student in the business school and that he was singularly focused on getting a job in the corporate world. Unfortunately, these conversations are often all too familiar to many of us who teach Black history. Some Black students simply find my class and other Black-centered courses to be lacking intellectual value. But when these same students see how many white students have enrolled in my course, they adjust their outlook and enroll as well.

If the attitude from the Black male student in the business school represents one type of hostility to Black history, then another type of hostility is expressed by some African-born students who were raised in the United States. Unfortunately, many African students at universities across the country were taught to look down upon and to not associate with African American students. "Dr. Moore, I was constantly told by my parents not to become like y'all." When I asked why, she stated, "Everything we see in Africa about Black people in America is bad. Y'all are lazy, y'all complain a lot, and y'all blame white people for everything. There are too many opportunities here in the United States but y'all don't take advantage of them." Her answer is so troubling because many African students and their parents are completely ignorant of the African American experience. Thus, there is no acknowledgement of or appreciation for the sacrifices African Americans have made to create the opportunities that African students and their parents have access to upon arriving in the United States.

For both African American and African students, the course provides them with a sense of pride, a sense of belonging, and a sense of identity. At the end of the semester I want the skeptical Black students to understand that because they now have a firm grounding in their own history, they are better equipped to navigate the turbulent waters of the real world. Similarly, I want African students to appreciate the African American struggle and to realize that the life experiences of Africans across the globe are interconnected.

The end of every fall semester brings mixed feelings. While I am excited about the Christmas break, I realize that I will not see this collection of students again. When

I finish the last lecture and thank them for taking the class, the students generally start clapping. As students say goodbye, I hope that over the past fifteen weeks I've done a good job of preparing them for the real world. As they pursue internships, full-time jobs, or graduate and professional school, they now have a certain amount of awareness about the Black experience in America that they will take with them to the marketplace. Being able to impact students through the teaching of Black history is the culmination of a dream that started during my high school years in Cleveland.

TEACHING
MYSELF

MY JOURNEY TO A CAREER TEACHING BLACK history began in Cleveland Heights, Ohio, a working-class, inner-ring suburb next to Cleveland. Growing up, it was about 40 percent Black, 30 percent white, and 30 percent Orthodox Jewish. Within a fifteen-minute walk from my parents' house, there were about three Jewish funeral homes, an entire Jewish business district with over thirty Jewish-owned businesses, the Jewish Community Center, about four or five synagogues and temples, and Park Synagogue, a mammoth facility that sat on more than thirty acres right in the middle of our neighborhood. I vividly remember seeing large groups of Jewish kids heading to Hebrew Academy and seeing yellow school buses with the words Mosdos Ohr Hatorah painted on the side, another Orthodox Jewish school. Little did I know how powerful those experiences would be for Jewish kids.

When I got older, I remember asking an older Jewish woman why they sent their kids to Hebrew school instead of the public school. Her response: "We will never let Gentiles educate our children again." She went on to mention how important it was for Jewish children to learn the history and culture of the faith and for them to never forget the Holocaust. Woven into that curriculum were clear sets of expectations for how women and men were supposed to act. I would see them walking up and down the street in traditional Orthodox Jewish dress and I found myself admiring it. They were proud to be Jewish, and they didn't care what anyone else thought. In many Black families and communities, we don't have the kind of academic and spiritual structure that teaches us about our history, lives, and culture. We grow up not knowing who we are. We learn about our history in a haphazard fashion: a Black History Month program at church, a Black history book report at school, the occasional Kwanzaa program, and older relatives reminiscing about the ancestors at the family reunion banquet.

I GUESS YOU CAN SAY THAT I WAS DESTINED TO BE-come a history professor because history is the only sub-ject I've ever enjoyed. When I finished high school with a 1.6 GPA in 1989, the only classes I earned higher than a C in were African American Literature and African Ameri-can History. I remember walking into the literature class in the eleventh grade and the teacher was a white dude who looked like Stephen King. But I didn't have a problem with him teaching it because the students loved him. He exposed me to H. Rap Brown, Stokely Carmichael, Angela Davis, and so many other luminaries from the 1960s. I was hooked. I took a Black history class the next semester and was disappointed. The teacher, who was Black, was never prepared, and hell, we didn't learn anything. She would always be eating fish sandwiches when she should've been teaching. I guess she was close to retirement, because she didn't take the class seriously. That summer, I would get on the bus and head downtown to the massive Cleveland Public Library. I would camp out in the Black history section for hours, and then I would look at microfilm copies of the *Cleveland Call and Post*, a Black paper, just to understand a bit more about Cleveland's racial history.

Nonetheless, when I enrolled at Jackson State University in the fall of 1989, I didn't even think about majoring in history. I was an education major primarily because at eighteen I had no idea what I wanted to do. But after sitting through an amazingly boring first semester of prerequisites, I changed my major to history, even though I had not taken a single history class. "What the hell you gonna do that for? You can't get a job majoring in that bullshit!" That was the response from my boy at Jackson State when I told him I was changing my major to history. But he wasn't done. "This nigga think he gone be W. E. B. Du Bois or Malcolm X or some shit. I told that nigga he need to take his ass down to the computer science building or get a business degree." And the criticism continued even among family. "What are you gonna do with a history degree?" I didn't know, but I was gonna major in it. "And Black history at that. Can't you pick a real major and then do Black history on the side?" It even continued at my church when I was approached by a longtime family friend who was in her seventies.

"You say that you are majoring in history and you wanna do something with Black history?"

"Yes, ma'am," I responded.

"I could see maybe European history, but not Black history," she said, shaking her head as she walked away. Despite the criticism, it was the best decision of my life, because I had some amazing professors, like Denoral Davis and Sheila Moore, a white woman who was woke long before anyone called it that.

As graduation approached, I figured I would go back home and get a job doing something. But one evening, while my boys and I were playing *Madden* at like 3:00 a.m., I noticed my friend filling out some papers.

"What are you doing?" I asked.

"Filling out these papers for grad school," he said.

"What's that?"

He said, "Like getting a master's degree or a PhD. I'm applying to go to grad school for school psychology." What's amazing is that although my aunt had a PhD in clinical psychology from Michigan and my other aunt had an EdD from USC, I was still clueless about graduate school. But I told myself, "I'm as smart as Brandon, so I'm going to grad school as well. I'm gonna get a master's degree in history." I got accepted into the only places I applied: Cleveland State University and Case Western Reserve University. The latter was my dad's alma mater.

Cleveland State gave me a graduate assistantship but they made it clear it was only for nine months, so guess what, I finished that degree in nine months. But I almost quit midway through the first semester. I was in a historiography class and we had to turn in a draft of a ten-to-twelve-page historiographical essay. I worked hard on that paper but when I got the draft back it had red all over it. It looked like blood had been spilled. While the comments were constructive, they were painful to read. It was clear I had to work on my writing. Although I almost quit the program, I stuck it out and ended up at Ohio State University in the fall of 1994 to begin working on my PhD in history with a specialization in African American history. I loved it and I killed it. I was among ten to twelve Black PhD students in the history department specializing in African American history. Upon graduating in 1998, I accepted a position at Louisiana State University as a history professor, and that is where I began teaching Black history to white people.

WHY I LIKE TEACHING BLACK HISTORY IN THE SOUTH

When I got to LSU a week before school started, I walked around campus passing out flyers about my classes. I went to the union, the Black cultural center, and the athletic facilities to recruit students. I wanted my classes to be full, but since I was new to the campus no one knew me. My efforts paid off, the classes were electric, and every semester after that I had long waiting lists of students wanting to get into my class. During my second year at LSU I fell in love with Thaïs Bass, who also loved Black history. She had majored in African American studies and English at the University of California, Los Angeles. We got married, she moved to Baton Rouge, and we became the "woke couple" on campus. My time at LSU showed me that the South is absolutely the best place to teach African American history. Let me say that again. The South is absolutely the best place to teach African American history. I was at LSU for nine years before taking my talents to the University of Texas at Austin in 2007. I find the South to be one of the only places in the United States where you can have an open and honest conversation about race. Let me provide a few examples of the experiences I have had with white people in the South.

My youngest daughter was in competitive cheer several years ago—and that is an expensive sport, by the way. We were at an event in San Antonio and I was engaging in small talk with another dad. He asked me what I did for a living and I told him that I was a professor at the University of Texas and that I held an administrative position within the Division of Diversity and Community Engagement. (Whenever you tell somebody white that you work in a division like that, there's usually an awkward pause.)

Later that afternoon he said, "Leonard . . . can I call you Leonard?"

"Yes."

He said, "Can I ask you a question? But I don't want to offend you." I've learned that if somebody prefaces a question with the idea that they don't want to offend you, then they probably are about to offend you. Then he proceeds to ask what he's been wanting to ask ever since I told him I worked at UT.

"My daughter is at Westlake High School and she's not in the top 10 percent. I don't think she'll be able to get into UT, but I think y'all are letting too many unqualified Black and Hispanic students enroll at UT." He continued, "If my daughter were at an inner-city high school, she'd be valedictorian."

My response was, "Well, if your daughter was at an inner-city high school, her whole experience would be different."

On another occasion I was invited to speak at an event in Lakeway, a wealthy suburb outside of Austin. Now, understand, they invited me to speak; I didn't invite myself. There were about ninety people in the room, all white men, and it was me and two of my Black male graduate assistants. I wanted them to share the experience and to provide me with some bodyguard protection just in case I needed it. As the leader of the event circulated my biography prior to my talk, between eight and ten people immediately got up and walked out, while a few others simply slid the biography away from them. I remember thinking, "Man, these guys are hard-core. I haven't even said anything yet and they're already mad." But I was not offended.

During my lecture I made it a point not to mention anything about race. I talked about the connection between globalization and higher education. I didn't mention anything about race, diversity, racism, or discrimination. When my talk was over, one of the men asked, "Dr. Moore, can we talk about Black Lives Matter?" Now, for the record, I hadn't said anything about Black Lives Matter, but that's what he wanted to talk about.

I said, "Since you want to talk about Black Lives Matter, we can go ahead and talk about that."

"If you all would just obey the police, you wouldn't get shot." He said it in such a bold and emphatic way, it was as if he had been waiting to say that for a long time. Now, that may be deeply offensive to some of you, but his statement is the reason I like teaching Black history in the South. Because when people come at you like that, you can have an open and honest conversation about race. He and I had a tense conversation for ten or fifteen minutes. In Texas and much of the South, the conversations are much bolder, people are less politically correct, and people don't care about your feelings.

One more example, just to further illustrate the point. Every year during Black History Month I spend a day at McCallum High School in Austin speaking to several classes. In February 2019, I noticed what appeared to be a parent in the class sitting next to his daughter. I'd seen this movie before. He was visibly disturbed throughout the entire presentation, and I knew he would approach me at the end of the class. He did. He told me that I needed to start including other viewpoints and that I needed to stop trying to poison kids against America. He then went on to tell me that he was going to send me some books to read so I could have a more "balanced" lecture. I simply checked him on his arrogance, his hubris, and let him know that his comfort in approaching me with this nonsense was a clear sign he needed to take an African American history course, and that he should be thankful his daughter attended a school that exposed all kids to Black History.

Last example, I promise. When my daughter was in middle school I participated in a career fair. Throughout the day I would visit classes and tell them about what it was like being a professor. In one particular class we started talking about police brutality and Black activism. I shared with the students my own experiences with police harassment, and my daughter talked about what it was like seeing her dad, me, being harassed by the police. The class appeared to enjoy the perspective my daughter and I shared. Except for one student. The next day I received a call from a parent who told me that I shouldn't be "up at the school teaching kids to hate the police." It took me a minute to realize what he was talking about, so after he finished talking, I asked him if he was a Trump supporter. There was an awkward pause. I then told him never to call me with this nonsense; if he didn't want his daughter to be exposed to different opinions, then he needed to homeschool her. After that, the conversation was civil and productive. He then went on to apologize for calling me and stated he hoped we could meet up at a later point to continue our conversation.

There is a belief among many Black folks that one of the first things immigrants learn when they come to America is to dislike Black people, and to dismiss the legacy of slavery, segregation, and racism. During the COVID-19 pandemic I did a ton of workshops and talks for corporations, associations, and other organizations, with those in attendance largely conservative white folks. Most of the feedback was overwhelmingly positive, but I soon noticed a trend. Many of the immigrants on some of these calls found my presentation to be problematic. One stands out above all others. After a session with a statewide realtor association, a member emailed me. Here are her words: "I was terribly disappointed at your presentation and I feel sorry for your students because you indoctrinate them to hate white people. Bringing up slavery and segregation does nothing but create division. I am a Chinese woman who grew up in Brazil and if I can make it in the United States then I know Black people can. But it is people like you who are holding this country back. You need to stop bringing up the past and then maybe Black people can appreciate this country for all of the opportunities we have." Yes, she actually took time out of her day to write this email, locate my email address, and hit send. You can't make this stuff up.

I BELIEVE IN THE POWER OF TEACHING. I REMEMBER when I was a graduate student at Ohio State and they gave me my own American history class to teach. I was excited. It was a winter quarter class that met on Monday evenings from six to nine. I remember on the first day of class a young man walked in wearing a tank top, and this is in early January in Columbus, Ohio. On his right bicep was a Confederate flag tattoo. Every Monday night he was there with his tattoo visible. I didn't know if he was trying to intimidate me or what, but at the end of those ten weeks, the young man approached me with tears in his eyes and said, "Mr. Moore, I never knew this about the Black experience.

I want to apologize to you for coming in here every day and showing you my tattoo." This is why I really believe in the power of teaching. I believe the more we know about the history of the Black experience, the more it will allow us to address racial tensions effectively.

This does not mean we teach a sanitized version of Black history. It means telling the good, the bad, and the ugly. We can't run from the ugliness of slavery, lynching, and the brutalizing treatment of Black people. When my kids were younger they hated watching movies about slavery and segregation. They would say, "It's too depressing. How can you watch that all the time?" Not only do we have to tell the ugliest of history, we need to sit in that ugliness and process it. For example, I will never forget my trip to the Holocaust Museum in Washington, DC. Although I grew up in a community with a vibrant Orthodox Jewish presence, I never understood the full horror of the Holocaust until I went to the museum. When it was time for them to close, I asked a staff member if I could stay longer and just lock up when I was done. The hours I spent in the museum digesting history and reading about people's experiences were life changing. If you ever visit, I guarantee that you will exit the museum absolutely speechless. This is how impactful history can be when done well. It is designed in many ways to change attitudes, perceptions, and viewpoints.

If history can be impactful, then why is the teaching of Black history controversial? The idea of even offering a Black history class can be contentious. Several years ago a Texas politician attempted to introduce a bill in the state legislature that was designed to lessen the popularity of my course on the Black Power movement—a class that routinely enrolls more than five hundred students.

Adding to the course's appeal is that it counts for an American history credit. So in an effort to minimize the course's popularity, a bill was drafted that would've eliminated the class from the approved list of courses that fulfill that American history credit. Thankfully the bill never saw the light of day.

Every February during Black History Month, I get invited to a number of high schools. Inevitably, I'm asked, "Dr. Moore, what are you going to talk about? The principal is kind of worried. The superintendent doesn't know if it's a good idea to have you come speak." Really? But why? Black history is a part of the fabric of American history. In the 1960s, when Black students were demanding Black studies courses at major universities, administrators routinely said no. I remind students about this history because it wasn't easy getting Black history into the curriculum. This still occurs in universities and high schools to this day. The state of Texas, for the first time in its history, only just now adopted African American studies as an elective in high schools. In 2019. In places like Cleveland, Detroit, Chicago, New York, Philadelphia, and Los Angeles, they've been teaching Black history in the high schools since the late '60s and early '70s. But the South has been slow to adapt.

As I look back on my experiences, I realize that not everybody is built to teach Black history to white people. But I am. I appreciate the challenge, the pushback, and the intense reactions. Throughout my career I've taught more than twenty thousand students, and more than 50 percent have been white. I believe that their experience in my class has been transformative. In June 2020, while watching many Americans demonize protestors and Black Lives Matter activists in the aftermath of the George Floyd and Breonna Taylor police murders, I told myself, "If they only knew the history of the Black experience then perhaps they would have a different perspective." Days later my team and I at the University of Texas at Austin decided to take my teaching beyond the traditional classroom to speak to a much larger audience of white people.

TEACHING
BLACK ANGER

I N AN EFFORT TO EXPLAIN TO WHITE PEOPLE WHAT they saw during the racial protests of summer 2020, I came up with a crazy idea. I told our staff I wanted to offer a ninety-minute webinar for the university community to help explain Black frustration. They were initially hesitant, but we all felt that the university needed a more significant response than just a statement from the president. We set a date, sent out the invites, and waited for the RSVPs. The title of the webinar was Managing in the Age of George Floyd and Breonna Taylor, because it was initially designed for those in leadership positions.

Within hours we had over one thousand RSVPs, and I received several emails and texts from colleagues saying they were looking forward to it. The RSVPs continued, and on the eve of the talk, we had over 4,200 people registered. Our Zoom account was maxed out, so we decided to simulcast on YouTube. "Forty-two hundred people!" I told my wife. That's almost one-third of the entire faculty and staff population at the university. I assumed more than 80 percent of the people who had RSVPed were white.

But there was one problem: I had no idea what to talk about. I woke up at 5:00 a.m. on the day of the event, and it hit me. I would have no slides, no PowerPoint, nothing. I would sit at my dining room table and speak. I knew I wanted to cover the following topics: Black frustration, the legacy of police brutality in the Black community, racial Monopoly, the civil rights framework of white people, and systemic and institutional racism. The webinar would close with seven practical steps white people could take to improve America's racial climate. I must confess I was nervous about this talk. I knew it would either go real good or real bad. I put on a suit and tie and then went to my dining room. I opened up the laptop, clicked on the Zoom link, made sure my camera was okay, and let loose. I needed to start by finding a unique way to show how the long legacy of racism affects Black people today. Enter racial Monopoly.

RACIAL MONOPOLY

When people make references to overt racism being a thing of the past, I remind them that the present is a product of the past, and I use the game of Monopoly to provide a clear illustration. I'm a big Monopoly fan, and while playing a few years ago, I noticed that the game could be used to explain the Black experience in America. (One quick Monopoly tip, buy all the railroads. With them, you'll never lose the game. You may not win, but you will never go bankrupt.)

So here's my Monopoly example: You are Black and are invited to a game of Monopoly with your white friends. As the banker is passing out the money, you realize everyone else has gotten $1,500 but you only received $800. You mention the discrepancy and they say, "It's in the rules."

You look at the rules and there it is: *Each Black player shall receive $800 at the beginning of the game.* You then pick a piece as your friend goes over the rules, reminding everyone that the goal is to acquire property, build on those properties, and then bankrupt your opponents. You've played Monopoly before, so you wonder why they felt the need to explain the game. But then they go over another rule that has a direct impact on you. You are told you cannot buy any property until you roll for the twentieth time. You've played Monopoly since you were a kid, and this rule sounds strange. You dispute it, but again they say, "It's in the rules." You look in the rules and there it is: *Black people cannot buy any property until they roll for the twentieth time, but they must pay rent and taxes and can go to jail.*

You still participate despite the unfair rules. When you finally get to your twentieth roll of the dice, you are excited. "I can finally buy property and make some money." But you notice all the properties have been bought. And no matter how hard you roll the dice, no matter how smart you are, no matter how good your negotiating skills are, you will never be able to compete. You are in a position of perpetual indebtedness, and there is nothing you can do about it. As you sit there and come to the realization that the game was structured for white people to win, someone says, "How come you don't have any property? You must be lazy, you must not want to work, you must want a handout." Your response: "The rules of the game were unfair." Then they'll say, "That was a long time ago. You just didn't work hard enough."

This is why African American history should be a graduation requirement in every high school, college, or university in America. Every. Single. One.

I am convinced that if we teach Black history in high

school, then the racial divide won't be so profound. But large portions of white America don't want it taught in schools. They don't want to dig up the sins of the past and acknowledge that racism didn't end with the civil rights legislation. They think that the 1964 Civil Rights Act and the 1965 Voting Rights Act effectively broke down all racial barriers in the United States. Despite the in-your-face evidence that racial injustice still exists, many people think that racism is just a figment of the Black imagination and that "playing the race card" is just a convenient excuse for Black pathology. If your racial framework suggests that racism is a thing of the past, then it is easy for you to reject terms like "systemic racism" and "institutional racism." How do these terms still affect the United States?

SYSTEMIC AND INSTITUTIONAL RACISM

The tragic murder of George Floyd shows how systemic and institutional racism works.

STEP 1. Officer Derek Chauvin had no problem putting his knee on the neck of an African American male for nine minutes and twenty-nine seconds, even though it was in broad daylight and people were recording. In Officer Chauvin's subconscious mind, the culture of the Minneapolis Police Department suggested he would not be punished or go to jail.

STEP 2. Although Mr. Floyd lay there unconscious, motionless, and lifeless, the officers never offered any medical assistance.

STEP 3. Officer Chauvin kept his knee on Mr. Floyd's neck for a full sixty seconds after the paramedics arrived.

STEP 4. The four officers at the scene when this occurred

lied on the initial police report by writing that Mr. Floyd was resisting arrest.

STEP 5. The day after the murder, the district attorney stated, "There is other evidence that does not support a criminal charge."

STEP 6. It took the district attorney's office seventy-two hours to indict the officers, even though there was video evidence.

STEP 7. When the officers were indicted, it was on lesser charges: a third-degree murder charge and a second-degree manslaughter charge.

STEP 8. The medical examiner's report stated that Mr. Floyd died from cardiac arrest caused by heart disease and hypertension, not through asphyxiation or strangulation.

These steps illustrate how the Minneapolis Police Department, the district attorney's office, and the medical examiner all conspired to protect one white man. Three separate entities worked together in an effort to ensure that Officer Chauvin would not be held accountable for the murder of Mr. Floyd. This is what we call institutional and systemic racism. This murder happened in a liberal state, in a liberal city, with a liberal mayor and a liberal district attorney. So if institutional and systemic racism are prevalent in liberal Minnesota, can you imagine what is happening in other states?

POLICE BRUTALITY

Many white Americans have this idea that police brutality only affects Black people in the hood. No, it affects every single Black person, regardless of income, education, religion, skin tone, or age.

As is true of many African Americans, the history of police interactions with Black people influences my choices. I generally avoid driving at night. Even when I'm on the highway in the daytime, I am conscious of how I am dressed. When I drive long distances, I put on a University of Texas Nike polo, a Texas Nike pullover, and a Texas Nike hat. I am literally a Texas Longhorns walking logo. That way, if I am pulled over, hopefully the police officer will assume I am a coach. The Texas Nike gear takes the focus off my Blackness and places it on the university. We can have a conversation about sports, the team, or the school in an effort to defuse any tension. I also have to be conscious of where I put my wallet when driving. I typically put it on the dashboard, but other Black men I know put their wallet in the trunk, so we can't be accused of going for a weapon when we are simply trying to retrieve our driver's license.

This issue doesn't affect only Black men. While my wife was a student at UCLA, she was pulled over many times by the Los Angeles Police Department. On one occasion, she felt that the officers were going to sexually assault her. What saved her? Her UCLA ID. It took the focus off her Blackness. Our experiences informed our decision to tell our two teenage daughters, "If a police officer pulls you over, pull into a gas station or to a public place that is well lit." This minimizes the chances of them being sexually violated by a rogue cop.

I want to share two interactions I've had in recent years with white police officers. Several years ago, I was driving on I-30 in Rockwall County outside of Dallas. A young police officer pulled me over at nine thirty in the evening. I was headed to Clarksville, Texas, and was going to stop at a hotel for the night. (Remember, I don't drive on the highway at night.)

"Officer, why did you pull me over?"

"When I passed you, you put your blinker on to change lanes, but you never changed lanes."

"You pulled me over for that?"

"Yes, we have to be careful out here because you never know." Then the officer asked, "Where are you going?"

"Well, I'm going to a hotel."

"Why are you up here?"

"I'm going to Clarksville in the morning."

"Why are you going to Clarksville?"

"I'm helping to try and get more of those kids to go to college."

"Are they paying you to go? Can you prove to me—do you have proof that you have a hotel reservation?"

"Officer, I have the reservation on my phone. Do I have permission to get my phone and scroll through the emails and show you the reservation?" I showed it to him. But the harassment continued.

"Mr. Moore, I need you to get out of the car because I need to search it for drugs and weapons." After doing a brief search of the car with his flashlight, he told me I could go but followed it with this: "Mr. Moore, thank you for letting me do my job tonight."

The second incident happened that same year, a few months later. I was stopped with my family in Bailey County, Texas, right inside the Texas border from New Mexico. It was me, my wife, and my three children, who were thirteen, eleven, and nine at the time.

"Officer, why did you pull me over?"

"Because when you changed lanes you didn't give the eighteen-wheeler in front of you enough space. You are supposed to have two car lengths between you and the next car when you switch lanes."

"That's why you pulled me over?"

"Yes. May I see your license and registration, please?"

"Do I have permission to get my license out of my wallet in my pocket and to look in the glove compartment for the registration? This is a rental car."

"Yes." After he looked at my license, he proceeded to ask a bunch of questions. "Where do you work?"

"I work at the University of Texas."

"You drive all the way from Round Rock every day to work."

"Yes, it's only about a thirty-minute commute."

"What do you do at UT?"

"I'm a history professor."

"How long you been there?"

"Ten years."

"Are you tenured?"

"Yes."

"When did you get tenure?"

"I was tenured when they hired me in 2007 from LSU."

"So, you teach history."

"Yes."

"What kind of history?"

"US history."

I knew he was going to dig deeper to see what courses I taught. There was no way I was going to tell this guy I teach a class on the Black Power movement and a class called Race in the Age of Obama. No way!

"So, you don't have a specialization. Most history professors specialize in something."

"Yeah, I teach Southern history." I was hoping he wouldn't go to his car and pull up my classes on his laptop.

"You said this is a rental car."

"Yes."

"What kind of car do you drive?"

"I have a Toyota Camry."

"What about your wife? What kind of car does she have?"

"She drives a Honda Pilot."

"What does your wife do for a living?"

"She directs a program at the University of Texas."

Then, after the questioning was over, it was on to the next and most serious phase of the harassment.

"Mr. Moore, I need you to get out of the car and go sit in the front seat of my police cruiser." Now, this is interesting. The dashcam points out of the windshield; it doesn't show anything that happens in the car. I was directed to sit in the front seat, where all the police gear is located, instead of the back, where most people are placed. There were two German shepherds behind me, and all I could think was, "Wow, all this officer has to do is pull out his gun and shoot me." His defense could simply be, "Mr. Moore went for my weapon and I killed him in self-defense."

I sat in the police car for fifteen minutes while my wife stood outside the rental car in tears. After fifteen minutes, the officer said, "You are free to go. Have a safe trip back to Round Rock." That's it. No apology. Nothing.

What do you think was the impact on my family? Not only on my wife, who unfortunately is used to it, but also on my three kids? Little kids, particularly boys, grow up idolizing people in uniform: firefighters, military, G.I. Joe, police officers. But do you know what it's like when your kids ask, "Daddy, I thought the police were good?" So much of how we as Black people prepare our kids for adulthood is to let them know that not all police are good. There are some who are rogue and racist and it is unfortunate that they messed it up for the good ones in their desire to maintain a racist culture of protectionism among white law enforcement officers. I've traveled to six of the seven continents, and the only place I've been terrified of the police is in my home country.

It was important for me to share these stories about police harassment with my white colleagues so they could see that Black folks don't just make this stuff up. The response to the webinar was phenomenal. I received countless emails and texts from colleagues, and that afternoon I told my team that we needed to take advantage of the moment. I brought up the idea of me teaching a Black history class to this same audience beginning the following week. "People are at home because of the pandemic and they have nothing to do," I remember saying. We set it up, I drafted a syllabus, and we registered over 1,300 people for the seven-week course. Now, obviously I wouldn't be able to teach the full scope of Black history in seven ninety-minute sessions, so I decided to pick out the most important parts of our history that best explain the contemporary Black experience to white people. The culmination of that effort is this book.

TEACHING ENSLAVEMENT AND EMANCIPATION

TEACHING CONTEMPORARY BLACK HISTORY STARTS with enslavement. My earliest memory about the history of slavery was watching *Roots* in 1977. I would sit in my parents' kitchen watching every episode on a twelve-inch black-and-white television. What I remember most is the music; it was fantastic. I don't recall much else, I just know it was on every night.

It wasn't until I got to college that I truly learned about slavery. Like many other Americans, I was largely clueless about the full scope of African enslavement in the United States. (A note on language. I don't use the word "slave." To refer to someone as a slave strips them of their identity and places them on the same level as a hog, a chicken, or a horse. Instead, I use the term "enslaved African" because it reminds us of their humanity and that they were people with feelings and emotions.) We learn so much American history in school, but we don't learn the truth about the creation of this country. I'm amazed when people argue that America was founded as a Christian nation. It wasn't. It was founded on racial slavery and capitalism. You can't be intellectually honest and disconnect them. They are intrinsically linked in this country.

WHAT CAME FIRST, SLAVERY OR RACISM?

The best place to begin a conversation about racial enslavement in the United States is to ask, What came first, slavery or racism? There's no definitive answer. Those who say slavery came first argue that enslavement is not endemic to the United States. It is an institution that has existed since biblical times. Those who take this side of the argument suggest that colonists developed a racial narrative or racist fiction to justify the enslavement of African people. On the other hand, those who argue racism came first suggest that preexisting racist attitudes among Europeans served as a catalyst for European exploration, the enslavement of Africans, and the eventual pillaging of African nations. So, although there is no consensus on this issue, many people believe racism came first.

What is not up for debate are the six distinct reasons Africans were enslaved in the United States. First, Europeans believed there was a seemingly endless supply of enslaved men and women in West Africa. Yes, slavery did exist in West Africa, and African elders and rulers routinely sold their own people and their enemies to Europeans in exchange for tobacco, gunpowder, and alcohol. Second, enslaved Africans were immune to many of the diseases in the North American colonies of Virginia, North Carolina, South Carolina, and Georgia. Many white indentured servants and colonists died from various sicknesses associated with the region's climate. Third, Europeans believed that through enslavement they would convert Africans to Christianity. Thus, being enslaved was actually a gift from God. Fourth, Africans were enslaved because they were skilled in agriculture. I ask students all the time, "Do you really think somebody from England went to South Carolina and knew how to set up a rice plantation? Or somebody from Wales went to Louisiana and knew how to set up a sugar plantation?" Furthermore, Africans were not only experts in agriculture but also gifted in skilled trades. You could find enslaved Africans serving as carpenters, coopers, shoemakers, tanners, and spinners and in a wide variety of other occupations.

The fifth reason Africans were enslaved is that they were not familiar with the geography. This is an important point. When Europeans attempted to enslave Native Americans, they were unsuccessful because Indigenous folks revolted and ran away. Since they knew the land, it was harder to find them. Comparatively, enslaved Africans weren't familiar with the surrounding territory, so their odds of a successful escape were slim. The last reason Africans were enslaved in the United States is because of the color of their skin. This is one of the reasons white indentured servitude didn't work. White workers could run away and blend in with the large free white population. But enslaved Africans could not run away without being easily identified.

People often defend the institution of slavery by stating that it has been around since biblical times. At this time, slavery existed in West Africa, but it was more of a domestic form. The distinction is that in the United States, slavery was racialized into chattel slavery. The enslaved were considered property and were enslaved for life. The slavery experienced in the former British colonies was arguably the most brutal in terms of damage done to people and to the African continent.

Racial slavery was woven into the fabric of this country; however, many people get offended if you refer to the founding fathers as "enslavers." I would add "hypocrites" to that description. As they were drafting the Declaration of Independence and the Constitution, they knew slavery was incompatible with those ideals. Given the chance to abolish it, they did the opposite. They threw the weight of the government behind it. In fact, the following "founding fathers" owned enslaved Africans:

George Washington
James Monroe
Patrick Henry
Thomas Jefferson
James Madison

So, what does the Constitution say about slavery and race? The Constitution mentions slavery in three articles. Article I, Section 2 deals with congressional representation. When the so-called founding fathers were discussing representation in Congress, there was a big debate over how enslaved Africans would be counted. With unmitigated gall, white Southerners said that enslaved Africans should count toward their population numbers. Northerners argued otherwise. They said that since enslaved Africans were considered property, they should not count toward the overall population of the South.

So they came up with a compromise. An enslaved African would count as three-fifths of a person. When Black people say "three-fifths" or "you only consider me three-fifths of a person," they are referring to the Constitution. Now, here's what I wonder: Why three-fifths? Why not five-sevenths? Why not two-thirds? Regardless of the answer, this article became the basis for how African Americans are treated in the United States of America.

The second place the Constitution explicitly mentions slavery is Article IV, Section 2. This deals with the issue of enslaved fugitives or runaways. If an enslaved African escaped to a free state they were still, in many ways, enslaved. The law went one step further by giving the enslaver the authority to bring back the enslaved African. The third place the Constitution references slavery is Article I, Section 9, which deals with the Atlantic slave trade. The article stated that in 1808, enslaved Africans could no longer be brought into the country. This section was ratified in 1793. What do you think happened in the fifteen years before it took effect? The slave traders brought in as many Africans as they could.

Slavery existed the longest in the Upper South states of Virginia, North Carolina, South Carolina, and Maryland. But we don't generally associate that part of the country with slavery. Before graduate school, if you had asked me where Frederick Douglass lived, I probably would've said Alabama, but he was from Maryland. I assumed that *Roots* was based in Mississippi, when in reality it was based in Maryland. Today, popular images of slavery are fixed squarely on the Deep South states of Alabama, Arkansas, Mississippi, Louisiana, Texas, Georgia, and Tennessee. When we review actual history, we discover that South Carolina was majority Black until 1790 and Virginia had the largest slave population from the 1600s until the Civil War. When you think about Virginia's proximity to Washington, DC, it becomes clearer that slavery and capitalism are inextricably linked in the fabric of this country.

The Louisiana Purchase of 1804 doubled the size of the United States and paved the way for King Cotton. Cotton was America's greatest asset from 1810 to 1860 and made the United States an economic giant. Without it there is no

Industrial Revolution. Historically, people have said that Eli Whitney's invention of the cotton gin paved the way for the lucrative staple crop. I learned about Eli Whitney in elementary and middle school, but no one ever made the connection between an enslaved African picking cotton in Mississippi, cotton shipped to New England to a textile mill, and the textiles used to make goods that would be sent to Europe. And did Eli Whitney really invent the cotton gin, or was it the invention of an enslaved African? I would argue that most technological advancements in agriculture prior to the Civil War were probably made by the people actually working in the field. We will never know the truth because enslaved Africans were not allowed to acquire patents for their inventions. When you hear Black people saying, "We built this country," this is what we are referring to. We understand the connection between capitalism and slavery. In 2004 the state of Louisiana created a new license plate to commemorate the two-hundred-year anniversary of the Louisiana Purchase. I remember looking at the license plate and thinking, "Wow, this event is nothing to celebrate. It was bad for Black folks and I don't want this on my license plate."

Cotton also impacted enslaved African families. Cotton cultivation requires 180 days of frostless weather. When Upper South slave owners saw how much money could be made with cotton, they sold their enslaved Africans "down the river" to the Deep South states. This trading in enslaved Africans was the domestic slave trade. If you go to New Orleans, Mobile, or Charleston, you can visit some of the places that used to trade enslaved Africans. Ironically, one of the original trading sites was located on present-day Wall Street, providing further proof of the connection between capitalism and slavery.

When we talk about the domestic slave trade, we use ballpark figures. One historian has said that the domestic slave trade involved over one million transactions. That doesn't mean one million people were sold; it means there were one million sales. People could be sold multiple times. Historians say that one-half of all the sales involved the destruction of a nuclear family. One-third of all sales involved the destruction of a first marriage. Cotton and the domestic slave trade separated spouses and families and changed the fabric of the American economy.

Let's talk about the pain of enslavement. I truly believe that Black people don't talk about the intergenerational pain enough. We talk about how our ancestors were resilient, how they built great communities, and how they survived. All of that is true, but we don't talk about the pain: the punishments, beatings, murders, and rapes and the physical, mental, and psychological torture. We need to acknowledge the horror of enslavement and how brutal the institution was and how the legacy still affects us. Part of the problem is that America glorifies plantation life and rarely mentions anything about white people enslaving, torturing, and murdering Africans.

Virtually every Southern state has a plantation you can visit, and Louisiana has the most. Just outside New Orleans you can visit several: Oak Alley, Whitney, Laura, Destrehan, and Evergreen. Evergreen Plantation is by far the most intriguing because it has fourteen original slave cabins at the back of the property. Louisiana is important to my journey of understanding enslavement and acknowledging the atrocities.

When I first moved to Baton Rouge in the summer of 1998, I was intrigued by the tours. I went on several of them, and although I didn't expect any serious discussion or analysis of the institution of slavery, I expected them to say something. On some tours, they didn't even mention the words "slavery" or "slaves." They would refer to enslaved Africans as "servants" or "workers." The tours usually centered on the architecture and furnishings of the house and how the plantation owners conducted their business and social affairs. On some of the tours the guides even dressed up in antebellum-era costumes. I soon realized that the story of enslaved Africans was not being told, so I started a company called Africans in Louisiana Tours in an effort to tell the other side of the story. During New Orleans's peak tourism periods, like Jazz Fest, Mardi Gras, and Essence, I would sell out of tickets and pack buses with up to fifty people to take them on my unique four-hour tour. How can we talk about plantation culture without mentioning the enslaved Africans who did the skilled and unskilled labor in southern Louisiana?

But the glorification of plantations does not end with tours. When I got to LSU in 1998, faculty and staff routinely ate in the Plantation Room. Thankfully, the name was changed years later and nobody had a problem with that. This term followed me when I moved to Austin, Texas. During our home search, my wife and I drove past a neighborhood called the Plantation that had a street named Plantation Drive. We just looked at each other. All throughout the South we have neighborhoods and restaurants with the term "plantation" in the name. It doesn't stop there. Throughout America are apartment buildings, housing communities, restaurants, streets, and more with the word "plantation" in the title. To illustrate how oblivious we are, I've got "plantation shutters" in my house.

Whenever I bring this up in public lectures someone often says, "Dr. Moore, 'plantation' refers to large farms during the antebellum period." I quickly respond with, "What made large farms during the antebellum period unique in American history?" The only distinction is that these farms were populated by enslaved Africans. It is impossible to separate the word "plantation" from enslavement. We have large farms now, but we don't call them plantations.

THE CIVIL WAR AND SOUTHERN WHITES

When we talk about the Civil War, we often fail to ask the obvious questions. Why would poor white Southerners fight for the Confederacy? Why would they fight to maintain a system that put them at a competitive disadvantage? What made them think they could compete economically in a region that had four million enslaved Africans providing free labor? The answer is that they fought because wealthy white Southerners constructed an elaborate narrative around white harmony.

At the top of the Southern social class sat wealthy slave owners with large plantations. Next were the yeoman farmers who might have owned one or two enslaved Africans. At the bottom were the poor whites. Prior to the Civil War, there were very few public schools in the South. The wealthy people did not want enslaved Africans and poor whites to learn how to read. They wanted to keep poor whites ignorant, uneducated, and poor so they could maintain control. There was no reason for the poor whites to join the Confederacy except for class (white) harmony.

In *Black Reconstruction*, the activist and scholar W. E. B. Du Bois talks about how wealthy Southern white people convinced the yeoman farmers and poor whites that they were all on the same team irrespective of income levels. The yeomen farmer believed if he worked hard enough, he could get a large plantation and own thirty, forty, or fifty enslaved Africans. Poor whites realized that the social and economic structure in the South prevented them from ever having enough money to purchase an enslaved African, but they took pride in the fact that although they were poor they were not enslaved. In essence they got a "psychological wage" from being white. What developed in the antebellum South was a culture in which people didn't talk about class interests. They were all white and united.

There are many books about poor and working-class white people and their political positions. Some argue that wealthy whites have manipulated lower-class white people, getting them to align with their race first as opposed to their economic interests. Isn't it ironic that many white working-class communities have such a disdain for government that they oppose the Affordable Care Act even though it would help them? In a sense they're willing to die for their political beliefs. Many rural Americans promote conservative politics despite these political leanings actually not benefiting them.

THE CIVIL WAR AND BLACK PEOPLE'S TRANSITION TO FREEDOM

One of the most misunderstood eras of the Black experience is the Civil War. Many people know that the Civil War led to the Emancipation Proclamation and that the war was fought over slavery. When we talk about the Civil War most people still believe that Lincoln freed the slaves. But the Emancipation Proclamation was issued partly due to military necessity. Whenever the Union Army got close to a plantation, enslaved Africans freed themselves and took refuge with the army. Over time this created a significant disadvantage for the Union Army because they had to take care of countless Africans who needed to be fed, clothed, housed, and protected. Lincoln signed the proclamation as a result. In addition, just because it was issued didn't mean that slaveholders and Southerners abided by it. It was only enforced when the Union Army got there. Many enslaved Africans in Texas did not know they had gained freedom, because the Union Army did not arrive en masse in Texas until June 19, 1865, two years after the proclamation was signed. This explains the Juneteenth celebrations, held mainly in Texas, when Black Americans celebrate freedom.

Formerly enslaved Africans made seven strategic decisions as they transitioned into freedom. These decisions provide a glimpse of what Black people were envisioning for themselves once slavery was over.

First, they left the plantation. Despite many antebellum ideas that enslaved Africans enjoyed being on the plantation, they wanted to get as far away from that traumatic environment as possible. Some might have spent their entire lives on the plantation, their relatives might have been buried there, but they also understood that it was a place of abuse, death, and terror. This was revolutionary because white Southerners had convinced themselves that enslaved African Americans enjoyed their condition and that they wouldn't go anywhere after emancipation. They thought freed Africans would still work on the plantation and still serve their former enslavers. While some did stay, many left, even if they didn't know where they would go.

Second, they reunited with their families as best they could. As mentioned before, the domestic slave trade separated families. After emancipation, it was challenging for freed Blacks to find their loved ones. Imagine that Leonard Moore is a formerly enslaved African living on a planation in Washington Parish, Louisiana. My wife, Dazettia, was sold from the plantation in 1857. I know nothing about where she was sold to. I only recall hearing that she was sold to Jackson. I can't pick up a phone, search a website, or even go to a courthouse to find out where she was sold to. There is no record, and I can't read, so the only lead I have is Jackson. In an effort to find my wife, I leave Washington Parish and go two hours away to Jackson, Louisiana. She's not there. Then I walk to Jackson, Mississippi. She's not there. I make my way to Jackson, Tennessee, but she's not there. Then I get on a horse and go to Jackson, Arkansas, and she's still not there.

Reuniting with family was deeply important to formerly enslaved Africans, but, tragically, it didn't always happen. People looked for their families or for spouses, only to find the latter and to realize they had remarried. Many people never found their families. Regardless of the outcome, these stories are powerful. Many people walked all throughout the South looking for their children who were sold away. The trauma associated with family separations affected subsequent generations of African Americans, and these stories need to be told. This is precisely why I believe that Black family ties appear to be stronger than white family ties. For instance, I rarely hear my white friends talk about their cousins or other extended family or even about having family reunions. Conversely, if you are Black and you miss two consecutive family reunions, your folks will remind you, "Don't forget where you came from."

Third, formerly enslaved Africans changed their names. My favorite Malcolm X interview was when somebody asked him about his last name and he said, "I don't know my last name because the names of our people were stolen in slavery." The reporter responded, "Isn't your last name Little?" Malcolm said, "No. Little is the name of the slave master who owned my grandfather." Just as it was to Malcolm X, the changing of the name was very, very important to formerly enslaved Africans. They no longer wanted to use the name of the slave master. When formerly enslaved Africans were changing their names, they chose ones that were familiar and had status. If you look at the names of the first five US presidents, Washington, Adams, Jefferson, Monroe, and Jackson, these names are now considered Black last names. I often wonder if white people with these names changed them as they became increasingly popular in Black America. I'm often asked why I still walk around with the last name Moore. A good friend told me that Moore is a British name and that I needed a name to accurately reflect the history and legacy of our people. I still reflect on that, but I think I'll keep the name Moore.

Whenever I conduct cultural intelligence workshops, one of the things I tell attendees is to never shorten somebody's name because it's convenient for you. We Americans disrespect others, particularly international people, all the time by asking if we can call them something else if their name is "too long" or "too hard" for us. We don't take the time to learn how to pronounce them correctly. We have to begin respecting people's names in America.

The fourth thing formerly enslaved Africans did was acquire land. When General Sherman conquered the South by marching through Georgia to the sea, he essentially broke the Confederacy and caused them to surrender. Once the Union Army occupied the states of Georgia, South Carolina, and North Carolina, Sherman hosted a meeting at the Green-Meldrim House in Savannah. A delegation of formerly enslaved Black men led by Reverend Garrison Frazier was invited, and Sherman asked them the following: "State in what manner you would rather live, whether scattered among the whites, or in colonies by yourselves?" Frazier's response to Sherman's question illustrated that they wanted to do for themselves. "We would prefer to live by ourselves, for there is a prejudice against us in the South that will take years to get over."

Largely based upon that meeting, General Sherman issued Field Order No. 15, known as Forty Acres and a Mule, on January 16, 1865. He promised the group that formerly enslaved Africans would get up to a forty-acre tract of land. A month later he threw in a mule and solidified that they would get land formerly owned by Confederates in Georgia, North Carolina, South Carolina, and along the coastal areas of the Upper South. Unfortunately, Sherman's order only lasted about four months. When Abraham Lincoln was assassinated, President Johnson rescinded the order, giving the land back to its former white owners.

The Forty Acres and a Mule policy is very, very important, because it represents a desire of formerly enslaved Africans. Even though it was overturned, some of them went and took over lands that had been abandoned by Confederates. The land was not very arable but they were able to eke out an existence. Sometimes they were able to purchase property after a year or two, but in either case, land ownership allowed them to have some degree of economic independence.

Number five, they built homes. Building a home was a clear sign that someone was now making freedom. Moving from slave quarters to one's own home was a revolutionary act, and it allowed a person to have somewhere to raise a family. Additionally, many Southern states have what were called "freedmen communities," communities built by formerly enslaved Africans in the years directly after the Civil War. Austin, Texas, was home to several vibrant communities, and ironically some of those communities are now hidden in some of the city's wealthiest areas because of gentrification.

The sixth strategy of making freedom was the establishment of schools. Before the Civil War, it was a capital offense in some places for a white person to teach an enslaved African how to read. Enslaved Africans who knew how to read and write often kept it hidden. They started schools because they knew the value of an education, and they also knew that education was powerful, since the enslaver had gone to great lengths to keep them ignorant on the plantation. When they started schools they had no desire for their children to be educated by white people. They created Black schools that would be staffed by Black teachers who would teach Black students.

And number seven, they started churches. They wanted to have their own religious experience. This is important, because on the plantation they were often subjected to a steady diet of sermons focused on obeying masters. But Africans had a different interpretation of Scripture. They didn't read the Bible from the viewpoint of the oppressor but from that of the oppressed. They understood that the Bible was meant to be viewed from the perspective of people living under Egyptian, Assyrian, Babylonian, and Greco-Roman oppression. They looked at Jesus as a revolutionary and a liberator and understood that the teachings of the Bible were not compatible with the institution of slavery. They realized that slave owners deliberately distorted the teachings of Jesus to fit their political and economic agenda. They had a totally different interpretation of what the Scriptures meant to them. They looked at the Bible as a liberating document, whereas the slave owner looked at it as a document to keep them in physical and spiritual bondage.

While formerly enslaved Africans were making freedom, they witnessed the passing of the Thirteenth, Fourteenth, and Fifteenth Amendments. The Thirteenth Amendment abolished slavery, the Fourteenth Amendment granted citizenship, and the Fifteenth Amendment gave all men, including Black men, the right to vote. But in the aftermath of these historic amendments, a troubling trend emerged. Whenever African Americans secured significant civil rights legislation, there was a visceral response and a vicious white backlash. There was a determined effort to erase the gains and to drive the formerly enslaved back into deeper levels of oppression. Enter Jim Crow.

TEACHING
JIM CROW

DURING THE YEARS IMMEDIATELY AFTER EMANCI-pation, white Southerners were completely terrified that their entire way of life was over. They confronted a world in which they were now part of a conquered nation. Their plantation economy was shattered, they had no political rights, and now four million formerly enslaved Africans were free. But as President Andrew Johnson began to restore some of their rights, many Southern states implemented a set of laws called Black Codes. The goal was to restrict the movement of formerly enslaved Africans and to get them back on the plantation.

From an economic perspective, if the cotton is not being picked or the sugar cane harvested, the regional economy dries up and the national economy suffers. So white Southerners established these obscene laws to get freed Blacks back on the plantation. The most grotesque part of the Black Codes were vagrancy laws. Many states mandated that African Americans have visible proof of employment by the first of every year. If they didn't, they would be in violation of vagrancy laws and sent to a plantation to work.

Some laws stipulated that African Americans could only work menial jobs and in agricultural work. Accompanying these restrictions were the proverbial "pig laws" that criminalized Black people for stealing chickens, hogs, and other animals. The punishment for breaking these laws was working on plantations.

This is what we talk about when we talk about criminalization. Many of the same issues that criminalized the formerly enslaved Africans still affect African Americans today. The Black Codes started a pattern in American history. Whenever African Americans achieved legislative victories, the opponents of Black progress found a way to keep Black folk in a position of servitude. So, despite the Thirteenth Amendment that abolished slavery, formerly enslaved Africans found themselves back on the plantation after emancipation.

I saw remnants of the plantation economy initially while a student at Jackson State and then years later while living in Louisiana. The first instance came during my freshman year, when my roommate, who was from Greenwood, Mississippi, told me he was gonna go home for the weekend and pick some cotton. He explained that he could pick cotton and they would pay him in cash based upon how much he picked. This sounded so outlandish that I didn't even know how to respond, but he said it with a straight face and without any shame. The second instance came while I was teaching at LSU and I was hired by the US Army Corps of Engineers to go to the Mississippi Delta. The army corps planned to build a bridge or a dam, but they'd found an old cemetery of enslaved Africans. They had to send someone to look at the historical nature of the cemetery before they could proceed with the construction. I flew into Jackson, Mississippi, drove to Greenwood, and then went eight or ten miles outside of the city to the location.

When I pulled up to the property it was surreal. There was a sign that said Sidon Plantation. And as I was driving on this large piece of property, I saw about six or seven Black men on a truck with the plantation name on the side of it. And I'm almost certain they were living on the plantation as well. The arrangement was very bizarre to me, and I got out of there as quick as I could.

During Reconstruction, African Americans held significant political positions at all levels of government. Fourteen African Americans served in the US House of Representatives and two in the US Senate. In various state government positions throughout the South there were hundreds of African Americans serving. The three states that had the most Black politicians were South Carolina, Louisiana, and Mississippi, with a total of about 1,500 Black Southerners serving in public office right after the Civil War. Since white Southerners could not vote or hold office, many Southern states ratified new progressive constitutions. These new constitutions called for the state to establish Black public schools, state hospitals, schools for the deaf and the blind, and a host of agencies designed to assist the poor. Their legislative priorities were rooted in their experience of being enslaved, and they understood in many ways that government should provide services for its residents.

But white Southerners could not and would not tolerate their new political and economic reality, and they took aim at the Thirteenth, Fourteenth, and Fifteenth Amendments. They wanted to nullify these amendments, to restore themselves as the political and economic elite of the region, and to get formerly enslaved Africans and their offspring back on the plantation. The Ku Klux Klan—established in Pulaski, Tennessee, in 1866—would usher in an unprecedented era of racial violence as it mounted a campaign to nullify the civil rights amendments through racial terror. From 1868 to 1877, there were untold acts of racial violence. One of the most famous incidents occurred in Colfax, Louisiana, on Easter Sunday in 1873. On that morning, between 70 and 150 African Americans were killed at the courthouse over a political dispute.

After the Colfax and similar massacres, the federal government withdrew from handling the South's racial problems in the Compromise of 1877. The Compromise of 1877 occurred after a disputed presidential election involving Rutherford B. Hayes. The Republicans agreed to pull all federal troops out of the South if Hayes was declared the winner of the election. The Democrats agreed, knowing that this would allow them to nullify all of the gains African Americans had made after emancipation and that it would allow them to hold power again. From 1877 to 1954, the federal government stayed out of civil rights issues in the South.

SEGREGATION: LEGALIZED AND INFORMAL

White Southerners in power moved quickly to restore the social order. But this period saw them introduce a social system that the American South had not seen before: segregation. During enslavement there was no need to separate the races because you had two classes of people: those who were white and free and those who were Black and enslaved. One group held all the power and the other group was considered nothing more than pieces of property.

After emancipation, white Southerners had to come up with a way to remind African Americans that they were inferior, worthless, no more than three-fifths of a person, and not equal to white people. They came up with this elaborate system of racial segregation that we call Jim Crow. Segregation meant separate schools, restrooms, libraries, recreational facilities, water fountains, movie theaters, cemeteries, and virtually every other area of public life. This directly impacted my family. My mother is from Franklinton, Louisiana. If you go there, you will discover that there is not a single public cemetery for Black people. The grave sites for Black people are in two places, either on the grounds of a Black church or in a private family cemetery. My family's cemetery is called St. James, and unless you know where it is, it is extremely difficult to find. My grandparents and a host of other relatives (including my uncle who died a few years ago) are buried there. When I walk through the cemetery I look at the tombstones and makeshift burial markers and realize that although Black Southerners were forced to create their own cemeteries, they are special and extremely sacred places.

Other institutions that were segregated included barbershops, parks, mental institutions, and schools for the deaf and the blind. Racial segregation even included textbooks. The textbooks that were used in the Black schools were kept separated in the book warehouse from the textbooks used for white schools. Furthermore, textbooks used in the American South often made no reference to slavery, democracy, the Constitution, or the Declaration of Independence.

There were also state-specific Jim Crow laws. One of the most unique laws was in Georgia and dealt with amateur baseball. The law said that Blacks and whites could not have baseball games within a two-block radius of each other. Hypothetically, if a game were happening on Seventeenth Street, then Black people couldn't play baseball on Fifteenth Street or Nineteenth Street. Also, the state of Mississippi passed a law that made it illegal for a Black motorist to pass a white motorist. It was believed that the dust from the Black person's car would fly up and hit the windshield of the white person's car, which would symbolize domination of Black over white.

In addition to legalized segregation, there were informal codes to Jim Crow. If they were broken there could be deadly consequences. Number one, a Black person was never to talk back to a white person, and Black folks were always to address a white person with the honorific Mr. or Mrs. Another informal code stipulated that if a Black person was walking on the sidewalk and encountered a white person, they had to get off the sidewalk and let the white person pass. Black people were also not allowed to smoke a pipe. Smoking pipes was reserved for white people and considered a habit for the upper class. If a Black person smoked a pipe, they were considered "uppity." Additionally, Black people were only allowed to wear nice clothes on Sundays; this explains why historically we have put on our best for church.

Another informal code of Jim Crow was that Black people were never allowed to approach the front door of a white person's house; they had to go to the back door. I witnessed this firsthand around twenty years ago. I went with a friend to pick up his mom, who worked as a domestic in the home of a wealthy white family in suburban Cleveland. When we pulled up to the house my friend just sat there and waited. I said, "Why don't you go ring the doorbell to let her know we are here?" He said, "Naw, I'll just wait." We waited awhile and finally he got out of the car and went to the back door and knocked. The culture of the work arrangement was that he would never go to the front door, only the back.

The informal codes of Jim Crow also forced intelligent Black people to act dumb. In the 1930s, Ivy League–educated Ralph Waldo Emerson Jones, president of Grambling State University, had to abide by this code whenever he went to the Louisiana State Capitol to lobby white legislators for more support for Grambling. He was well educated, a phenomenal university president, and wore suits every day. When he went to visit white politicians, however, he would change his appearance. He'd go to a friend's house, take off his suit, put on overalls and work boots, put some tobacco in his mouth, and head off to the state capitol.

When asked why he did that, President Jones said that if he showed up with a suit on, in a nice car, the white politicians would stop supporting his institution. He had to give the impression that he was an ignorant Negro so that they would not see him and Grambling State as threats to Louisiana's social order. He feared that if they really knew how well Grambling was educating its students, the state would actually close the institution. This speaks to a larger idea that if you are Black and have nice things, such as a car or a house, then you need to conceal it from white America. This is still profoundly true in 2021.

These informal codes were enforced by law enforcement and white private citizens. Black people had no standing in the courts. In many ways, they acquiesced to these informal codes because they understood they could be brutalized, assaulted, or murdered for the slightest offense to a white person. It was the informal codes that got Emmett Till lynched in 1955.

ELIMINATING THE BLACK VOTE

Once the former Confederates were back in power, they moved quickly to nullify the civil rights amendments by drafting new state constitutions. What is interesting about these new state constitutions is that they make no mention of race, but all throughout you can see that the language in many ways has a racial intent. And the racial intent is clear, considering that the sole purpose for drafting a new constitution was simply to disenfranchise Black people. Southern state legislatures came up with a variety of ways to keep Black folks from exercising their right to vote.

The first method was a poll tax. People had to pay a certain amount of money to be able to vote. For example, if you were a cotton picker in Coahoma County, Mississippi, you might make three dollars a week, twelve dollars a month. If the poll tax was four dollars, that was one-third of your income for a month. The poll tax was the barrier that kept poor Black people and all Black people from voting, because it was excessive. Another method to keep Black folk from voting was the literacy test. People had to show the voting official that they could read and write. The voting registrar would have questions for prospective voters to answer as proof. One question might be, "Give me the first, middle, and last name and birth date of everybody in Abraham Lincoln's cabinet." Another question might be, "Name every county in the state of Alabama." They might even ask "How many bubbles are in a bar of soap?" Or they might hold up a jar full of jelly beans and ask, "How many jelly beans are in this jar?" These questions were difficult or absurd. The literacy test applied to all Black people, but it could be used against poor whites as well.

The third piece of legislation used to prevent Black people from voting was the grandfather clause. The grandfather clause stated that if your grandfather couldn't vote, you couldn't vote. Many African Americans could not meet this requirement due to enslavement of themselves or their ancestors. Residency laws also served as barriers to Black political participation. Residency laws stated that people had to live in the same place for a period of time to be eligible to vote. This was problematic for many African Americans because of sharecropping. Sharecroppers often moved around looking for better deals and better economic arrangements, meaning they would not meet the residency requirement. Somewhat related to the residency laws were property requirements. In some places people had to be property owners to vote. The state of Texas had another way of limiting Black voter participation, and this was through the white primary. Black people could vote in the general election but not the primary. This was problematic because if the candidates for the primary election were all white supremacists, then it made no sense for Black voters to participate in the general election. This was legal in Texas until the 1940s.

Finally, white Southerners used violence and intimidation. In 1947 US Senator Theodore Bilbo of Mississippi was asked about ways to keep Black people from voting. His response was given on the floor of the United States Senate: "I'm calling on every red-blooded American who believes in the superiority and integrity of the white race to get out and see that no nigger votes. And the best time to do that is the night before!" The majority of white Southerners agreed with him.

Although these laws made no mention of race, they had a racial intent. This is not a relic of the past. There has been a resurgence of election laws that target African Americans, although the laws do not explicitly refer to race. For example, during Barack Obama's two presidential campaigns, Black voters in Cleveland made good use of early voting and worked with local churches around an event called Souls to the Polls. These organizations would park school and coach buses outside churches on Sunday afternoon so when services were over, folks would get on the bus and vote. This effort led to high rates of Black voter participation. Upon realizing the effectiveness of these efforts, however, Republicans in Ohio were successful in outlawing early voting on Sundays. The reason they gave was that poll workers needed a day of rest. It was a law that made no mention of race, but it had a racial intent. Fortunately, it was overturned in the courts.

I often argue that no single piece of legislation ever had such an immediate and noticeable impact as these efforts to disenfranchise Black voters during the Jim Crow period. Let's examine the state of Louisiana, which in 1896 had 103,000 Black voters registered. By 1903, just seven years later, there were only 1,300 Black registered voters. When Black folks in Louisiana were disenfranchised around the turn of the twentieth century, they did not vote again until the late 1960s. My grandmother lived her entire life in Louisiana but she never voted. She was born in 1920 but never registered or went to vote. Even in the 1980s, 1990s, and 2000s, she never voted. She always said that Black folks "didn't have no business voting." I often wonder what made her say that and whether it was because of what she had witnessed when Black folk attempted to exercise their right to vote.

Imagine how unfair life would be if you were paying taxes like everyone else but you couldn't vote. Black people in the South were effectively disenfranchised for sixty to seventy years, depending upon where they lived. They paid taxes but didn't get the benefits of saying where those taxes were used. Could one approach to reparations be that white Southerners have their vote taken away for sixty years to allow Black people to catch up or to level the playing field? Just think about that for a minute. If whites in Texas, Mississippi, Louisiana, and other states were disenfranchised for eighty years, how much progress could Black people make in terms of education, business ownership, career advancement, and political power? It would be considerable. But how would this proposal be received by the public? People would laugh and call it absurd—rightfully so. But this is what went on in the American South. People were paying taxes, but they never got any benefit from the taxes they were paying.

In some parts of the South, particularly in majority Black counties, Black taxpayer money was going to fund white endeavors. The parks, libraries, and public schools were not open to Black residents because of segregation. Some Black folks argued for having Black tax dollars in one pot, white tax dollars in another pot, with each pot used to fund endeavors for the individual groups. That sounds like a logical solution to me. But white Southerners would never agree to such a proposal because there would be less money for their endeavors. All of these policies gave white people a head start on economic, political, and educational advancement. When Black people were finally able to vote in the 1960s, they were not able to compete at the same level because of the years of disenfranchisement.

SHARECROPPING AND CONVICT LEASING

The primary economic system during the Jim Crow period in the American South was sharecropping. Sharecropping was an economic system that kept formerly enslaved people in perpetual indebtedness. But they were initially optimistic that this system would work for them. Here is why. They didn't want to live on a plantation, to work for a wage, and to have an overseer telling them what to do. That would be just like slavery. Instead they rented land from white landowners (generally former enslavers), planted crops, and gave a share of the crops as proceeds. The arrangement was supposed to help the formerly enslaved people, but in practice it was arguably one of the most atrocious forms of white economic exploitation that Black people have confronted, save for slavery. The sharecropper would have to get all the equipment, grain, seeds, and mules from the landowner, usually through a loan. The sharecroppers would work the land, but when the crop came in they would have to "settle up" with the landowner. Many sharecroppers were told that they worked hard but they came up short on their loan. If they came up short, they had to work another year to pay off the debt.

The system was white exploitation. There are stories of landowners charging 60 to 70 percent interest on goods. The landowner was keeping all the books, and many sharecroppers didn't know how to read, write, or do math. This became a system of perpetual indebtedness. Many states had laws that if you owed somebody money, you couldn't leave the county. It kept Black sharecroppers on the plantation year after year, while white landowners reaped the benefits of Black labor. What had started as a system that Black people embraced because it gave them autonomy turned into an economic and social nightmare that some never recovered from. So, were there white sharecroppers too? Absolutely. Were they being exploited? Yes. But at the end of the day, they were still white. They had an element of privilege over poor Black people. In issues dealing with

Black-versus-white relations, poor whites had some security that the system would support them over a Black person, even if that Black person were their peer.

The legacy of Jim Crow is sometimes so insidious that we don't recognize it. About twenty years ago two African American residents of Houston discovered that one of Houston's most prosperous suburbs, Sugar Land, was formerly home to a notorious convict-leasing camp. In an effort to get Black men and women back on the plantation, many states launched convict-leasing programs. They would convict Black men and women of frivolous crimes, but instead of sending them to jail or to prison, they would lease them out to a landowner. Throughout the South, convicts worked on railroads, on plantations, and in factories. Why were Black people convicted of and sentenced for minor crimes? Because there were plantations that needed to be worked. You come up with a bunch of laws that Black people are going to break, you convict them of the crimes, and you send them out to landowners. You do it as a political favor, but also so the state does not have to spend money building prisons.

The average lifespan of convicts, once they were leased out, could be rather short. It's arguably worse than slavery, because in slavery, the enslaver had a personal, financial investment in African Americans. With convict leasing, there was no investment whatsoever. Landowners would work the Black convicts to death. When they died, the landowners could request more convicts from the state. There was a seemingly endless supply of Black convict labor.

Convict leasing increased in popularity because it was a win-win for everybody white: the economy was growing again, the state did not have to build a prison, and landowners had people back on the plantation working. As the demand for convicts increased, it soon exceeded the supply. What did Southern politicians do to meet the demand? They began to criminalize an entire race of people to get them on the plantation to work. When Black people talk about the criminalization of an entire race of people, this is what they are referring to. Around the same time, social science literature began to talk about how Black people were inherently criminal. In many ways the criminalization was supported by research.

LYNCHING

One of the interesting things about the Black experience during Jim Crow was how public white Southerners were in their racist treatment of Black people. This extended to lynching as well. Although we don't teach about lynching in school, we need to. In fact, we should dedicate an entire week to a serious discussion of lynching and how it impacted both Black and white communities. Although the majority of people lynched were men, Black women were lynched too, often as they tried to save their sons. Since most of us have easy access to the internet, please google the lynching of Will Brown. I will reference his lynching in this next section. I need to warn you that it is graphic, yet at the same time it is part of American history. When you google the lynching of Will Brown, you will see countless other images of people being lynched. Why? Because there was a cottage industry called lynching photography. Photographers would go to a lynching, take a picture, and create a postcard with the image. That's why we have so many of them.

Now let's look at the lynching of Will Brown in Omaha, Nebraska. If you look at the photo you will notice a number of things. Number one, nobody is hiding their face.

They are posing for the photograph. Some people are even smiling. There is also a young kid posing for the picture. Next, notice that they appear to be well dressed. There's a large crowd. It appears to be a spectacle. And it is obvious that there aren't any Black people in the photograph besides Mr. Brown. Now look at Mr. Brown, who has been lynched. His intestines are exposed. He was burnt alive in what they called a "Negro Bar-B-Q." This is American history in all its ugliness. These are the chapters of American history that mainstream America either doesn't know about or, in many ways, wants to forget. My philosophy is we have to show the good, the bad, and the ugly. Tell the whole story. In some places, people would be offended at the photograph. They would say it creates too many problems. But we have to get to a point where we can acknowledge our nation's history, because that is the only way we will be able to move forward.

This is all part of American history. What enforced the informal Jim Crow laws, what enforced order, was things like this. Lynching, convict leasing, and other forms of control impacted not just one generation of people but sometimes two and three generations. It influenced the psyche because the message was, If you get out of line, this could happen to you. On the flip side, the message that was sent to the white kid in the picture was, This is what we do to Black people if they get out of line. They are not hiding their faces because, in their minds, they aren't doing anything wrong.

One of the most notorious and well-chronicled lynchings during the Jim Crow period was that of Sam Hose, who was burned to death in Georgia. If you read accounts of that event, you will see that when the local authorities accused Sam Hose of killing his employer, the editor of the *Atlanta Journal* wrote, "We will capture him and we will burn him alive." They caught him in Atlanta, took him to Griffin, Georgia, then decided to burn him alive in Newnan, Georgia.

Many lynchings were public spectacles, and the Sam Hose lynching was one of the most notorious. An account by the anti-lynching crusader Ida B. Wells talks of special trains from Atlanta to Newnan to bring people to the lynching. One of the reasons they moved it to Newnan was because the trains were not running on Sunday from Atlanta to Griffin. They took him to Newnan because they could get people on a train in Atlanta to see this Negro being burned alive. At the train station in Atlanta one of the porters would say, "Special train to Newnan, all board for the burning. Special train to Newnan, all board for the burning." Another train was chartered later that afternoon to accommodate those who wanted to attend the lynching after church. There were reportedly more than two thousand Atlanta citizens who went to Newnan, Georgia, to see Sam Hose murdered.

Sam Hose could not just be killed, his body had to be mutilated. At the scene of the lynching the mob cut off his ears, skinned his face, cut off his fingers, gashed his legs, cut open his stomach, and poured out his intestines. And they took his bones and body parts as souvenirs. One observer said, "They fought over the burning body, seeking souvenirs. Large pieces of flesh were carried away. Persons were seen walking through the streets carrying bones in their hands. Others scraped up the ashes." And then, "they even took the stake he was tied to. It was promptly chopped down and carried away as the largest souvenir of the burning." This is barbarism. They were doing this stuff in broad daylight.

But Sam Hose was not unique. You can look through the newspapers in Atlanta, Charlotte, Jackson, Mississippi, and many other Southern cities and see articles about planned lynchings. "Negro to Be Lynched" or "Negro to Be Lynched Tomorrow" were headlines in major papers. Here's my question: Why so much hatred? Why not just kill them? Why this spectacle? Why this performance? Why this theater-like atmosphere? Because they wanted to send a message to the African American community that this could happen to you if you got out of line.

"Negro Lynched in Louisiana Jail" is the headline of an article from the January 6, 1935, edition of the *New York Times*. The article is about Jerome Wilson, who was lynched in Franklinton, Louisiana. Why is Jerome Wilson important to this story? He grew up with my grandfather and my great-uncles, and they were distant cousins. They went to the same school, attended the same church, swam in the same creek, and lived in the same small Negro hamlet of Clifton. During a dispute over a mule at the Wilson family home, a Washington Parish deputy ended up dead, along with Jerome's brother. That evening all nine members of the Wilson family were in jail. Months later Jerome was dragged out of jail at three o'clock in the morning. He was beaten in the head with a hammer before being shot and killed. They then put him on the back of a truck and dumped his body in front of the Wilson family home, not far from my grandparents' house. His body was discovered by his twelve-year-old sister as she was walking to the bus stop to go to school. When the Washington Parish sheriff was asked about the lynching, he said, "There wasn't any lynching. Some men got into the cell somehow between 3 or 4 o'clock in the morning. They shot Jerome Wilson, apparently because he kept crying for help. They then sawed thru the lock of Jerome's cell. Someone beat Jerome over the head with a big hammer and left the hammer in the cell. They took his body out and threw it on the road. There wasn't any lynching. There wasn't any mob either. There were just about six or eight who were going about their business." To this day, nobody has ever been convicted for the lynching of Jerome Wilson. My mom was born three years after this happened, and she vaguely remembers family and community members talking about it. It was rarely talked about because the lynching instilled fear in a once vibrant African American community. At one point, Washington Parish had one of the largest percentages of Black landowners in the United States.

Although we don't teach about lynching in school, we need too. But here's why we don't teach about it. First, white parents don't want it, and second, there are some Black parents who don't want it taught either. I've been in-volved in a lot of conversations with white principals and white teachers who say, "Dr. Moore, we tried to introduce a Black history lesson that we felt was very appropriate, but we got calls from Black parents saying that their child felt uncomfortable." Then, on the flip side, you get white parents calling the principal saying, "Why are you teaching Black history? It should be American history." So school administrators often get resistance from both Black and white parents. Well-meaning principals want to diversify the curriculum, but then they get criticized. So to avoid controversy, they end up doing nothing.

BLACK INSTITUTION BUILDING

One of the ironies of African American history is that although Black people were confronted with lynching, sharecropping, convict leasing, disenfranchisement, and segregation, they did an unprecedented amount of institution building. Many of those institutions are still around today. More than 90 percent of the country's historically Black colleges and universities (HBCUs) were founded during this period, as well as the majority of African American church denominations, such as the National Baptist Convention and the Church of God in Christ. Additionally, Black Americans established a host of civil rights and professional organizations, including the following:

- National Association for the Advancement of Colored People (NAACP)
- National Urban League
- National Association of Colored Women
- National Council of Negro Women
- National Negro Business League
- National Colored Teachers Association
- National Bar Association
- National Dental Association
- National Medical Association
- National Bankers Association

They founded numerous other professional organizations to meet the needs of entrepreneurs and business owners.

Despite the terror, the lynching, and the disenfranchisement, Black people built communities, because they understood that they had essentially no legal protections. When my mom got married in 1959 and moved to Cleveland, she said she was disappointed. She had heard about how great the North was, but when she got there she said, "These folks don't have nothing." She grew up in a vibrant all-Black world, in a small rural community in Louisiana, with all-Black institutions that helped insulate her community from the terror of Jim Crow. There wasn't something similar in the North. Among her and her ten siblings, only three of them left the Deep South and migrated north: she and her two oldest brothers. Although some Black folks deemed the segregated South backward, she didn't; she took pride in being from the country.

Of all the areas of Black life that managed to flourish during segregation, the most prominent were Black businesses. The segregated Black community housed a vibrant Black business ecosystem in which Black folks spent their money with each other. The Black dollar was recycled through other Black-owned enterprises. But Black economic independence and prosperity were seen as direct assaults on segregation, ones that needed to be suppressed. The Tulsa Race Riot is a prime example. Black Tulsa had such a vibrant Black business district that it was often referred to as Black Wall Street. In 1921, however, it was burned completely to the ground by whites seeking to avenge the alleged murder of a white woman by a Black man. The Black community was not able to rebuild it to its former size and influence.

THE BIRTH OF CONFEDERATE MEMORIALS

As Black people were fighting Jim Crow and building institutions to insulate themselves from white terror, Confederate monuments and memorials were being erected in the South and in front of many county courthouses. Prior to the 1900s you would rarely see any Confederate statues or memorials. But as Confederate veterans began to die, many of their friends, relatives, and sympathizers felt that their military contributions would get ignored or erased. The United Daughters of the Confederacy decided to memorialize them and, in the process, to basically rewrite the narrative of the Civil War. They introduced the Lost Cause ideology into American history. This interpretation argues that the Confederacy was a heroic effort. The Civil War had nothing to do with slavery; it was about protecting the Southern way of life and about states' rights. The narrative also makes the argument that the Confederacy didn't lose the war. They were just overwhelmed by Northern aggression as they defended their Southern honor. This is pure fiction. Despite efforts to suggest that the war was not about slavery, it clearly was. The secession documents clearly state that these Southern states were leaving the Union because they wanted to preserve the institution of slavery.

Today you can find Confederate memorials and statues in more than thirty states. When you consider that there were only eleven states in the Confederacy, there was obviously support for these memorials in the Midwest and the Northeast. In 2021 there are ten military bases named after former Confederates, and there are Confederate memorials inside the US Capitol Building. The Lost Cause ideology is all about rewriting the history of the Civil War and the Confederacy.

This is why people will defend keeping Confederate statues and Confederate memorials in public spaces. While visiting Louisiana a few years ago in an effort to find the grave of one of Jerome Wilson's killers, I visited several white cemeteries. Many of the graves had C.S.A. (Confederate States of America) etched on the tombstones. On some of the graves, there were what seemed to be newly placed Confederate flags. So this history is still alive and well.

Although some Confederate statues have been removed because of Black activism, the overwhelming majority of them are still visible throughout the American landscape.

I am not necessarily in favor of removing Confederate statues. Instead I would prefer that we contextualize them, like what was done in some parts of Europe with Nazi statuary. I firmly believe that these memorials are better suited to a museum than to a public space. The contemporary battles over Confederate statues make it clear that we can't deny the impact or the importance of statues and these symbols. If they weren't important, they would not have been erected, and if they weren't important, people would not fight against their removal. Many white Southerners have been indoctrinated in Lost Cause ideology, so they will fight to the death to keep those monuments in the public sphere.

TEACHING
BLACK URBANIZATION

IKE ANY OTHER GROUP OF PEOPLE, AFRICAN
Americans were always looking for ways to better their
situation as they suffered in the throes of Jim Crow.
In the years after World War I and World War II, African Americans decided to pick up and leave the South
and head to the North, Northeast, and Midwest for better
economic opportunities. History talks a lot about white
people moving to the West to get property and expand the
United States. The Great Migration of African Americans,
however, was the largest internal migration of people ever
in the United States.

We use two terms when talking about migration:
push factors and pull factors. By push factors, we mean
the things pushing African Americans out of the South.
The push factors are easy: violence and terrorism. They
can't make any money. They can't express themselves as
true men and women. But also, a boll weevil attack triggered a sort of depression in the Deep South in terms of
agriculture. Since they weren't making much of a living
as sharecroppers, as tenant farmers, and through small

landholdings, they began to look at other places to go. The pull factors, things that were pulling them to the North, were economic opportunity, freedom, and hope. When Black Southerners left the South, they headed to Chicago, Detroit, Cleveland, New York City, Boston, Philadelphia, St. Louis, Milwaukee, Indianapolis, and other parts of the Midwest and Northeast. For them, it was as if they were entering a completely different country.

Roughly one million Black folk would leave the South from 1920 to 1930, with up to five hundred migrants a day arriving in New York City and Chicago and a couple hundred a day arriving in Cleveland and Detroit. But the Great Migration did not occur in a vacuum. At the beginning of World War I, the United States basically cut off all immigration in the name of national security. This created a severe labor shortage in many factories in the Northeast and Midwest because large numbers of white men were off fighting. To address the labor shortage, industrialists targeted Black workers in the South, not because they particularly wanted Black labor but because that was the only labor pool available. My paternal grandparents, Ezekiel Moore and Bessie Lee Moore (née Patterson) migrated to Indianapolis from Mississippi with their parents in the immediate aftermath of World War I. Grandma Bessie, as we called her, was a child prodigy. She became a concert pianist at age fourteen and then at fifteen was valedictorian of the class of 1930 at Crispus Attucks High School, arguably the best high school of any kind in America. My grandfather worked at the post office and played in a jazz band before he became a Holiness preacher. Together they would have thirteen children. Like other families, the Moores would migrate more than once: first from Indianapolis to Cleveland in 1944 and then from Cleveland to

Los Angeles in 1961. Although the Lord told my grandfather to go to Los Angeles, I often joke that it was the free California college tuition that sent them there. Of the thirteen children, my dad and his next youngest brother were the only two who stayed in Cleveland.

Black families did not always migrate as a unit. At times, the father would go north to secure lodging and employment and then would come back or send for the family. How did migrants determine where to go? A couple of things determined one's destination. Number one was a family or hometown connection. In Cleveland, we were part of a large network of people from Franklinton. On one occasion they had a cookout with almost one hundred people in attendance, and my mom knew literally everybody there. I remember asking her one time if she could recall the first person who had moved from Franklinton to Cleveland. She said she believed it was one of her distant cousins, who moved in 1933. Every time he came back to Louisiana, he would tell his friends and his family about the opportunities in Cleveland. Those who were interested would migrate to Cleveland and connect with him upon arriving. I often knew when my mom was talking to someone from Franklinton because her voice would be different. It was as if she were transported back home. Despite living in Cleveland from 1959 until her death in 2018, she always referred to Franklinton as home.

Some truly amazing stories came out of this large internal migration of Black folks to the North. One of the funniest stories involves Newark, New Jersey. Newark is just across the bridge from New York City. From Newark you can see the New York skyline and vice versa. In her book *The Warmth of Other Suns*, Isabel Wilkerson says that when migrants were coming from the South, a lot of them got off in Newark, New Jersey, thinking that it was New York City. Consider that if you are from Louisiana, Mississippi, Texas, or any other Southern state and the train conductor says, "Next stop, Newark," it is easy to assume the conductor is saying "New York." She writes that this was how Newark became a focal point for Black migration. Another great story involves migrants out of Louisiana, who usually went west as opposed to north. Apparently, if you had a good car you would drive all the way from Louisiana to Los Angeles. If you had a so-so car you went from Louisiana to Houston. If you had a broken-down car you went just across the state line to Beaumont, Texas.

If there was no family or hometown connection, male migrants would follow the train lines. Amtrak has a train called the City of New Orleans that runs from New Orleans, through Mississippi, and up to Chicago. When I was going to school at Jackson State University, a lot of us from the North were going to HBCUs in the South. For one, it was cheaper, and two, many of us had relatives in the South. I remember every Thanksgiving or Christmas break, I would hop on the train in Jackson, Mississippi, and it would be filled with HBCU students attending Dillard, Xavier, Southern, Alcorn State, Jackson State, and other schools. We were all headed back to Chicago, Detroit, Cleveland, St. Louis, or Milwaukee because our families lived in the North. The Chicago folks would get off and the rest of us would have a layover to take us east to Cleveland, Detroit, Philadelphia, and New York City. Even as a college kid in the early 1990s, I saw how the Great Migration really impacted Black life in terms of where we went to school.

Black business owners and pastors faced a dilemma during the Great Migration. They had to figure out how to respond when people left, because that was their clientele.

Black business owners had a couple of options: number one, convince their family members and clients to stay, because that was the source of their business; or two, close up shop and migrate with the goal of reopening their business in the North. Let's use a hypothetical example. Assume I am the pastor of St. James Missionary Baptist Church in Clifton, Louisiana. Now consider that during the Great Migration half of my congregation moves up North, with a good percentage of them moving to Detroit. There is a good possibility that I will move to Detroit at some point and start a church and name it St. James Missionary Baptist Church Number 2. It would be "Number 2" because this church is now the sister church of the original.

WHITE RESISTANCE TO THE GREAT MIGRATION

White Southerners did not just sit back and watch Black folk leave. That was their labor force. Furthermore, white elites also understood that to preserve white class harmony, poor white people needed the presence of African Americans so that they had somebody to look down upon. When Black folks started leaving, white Southerners came up with the Southern repatriation movement, with the goal of getting Black people to stay or to come back to the South.

The first way they tried to keep them was through violence and direct intimidation. At times white landowners would show up at the train station with guns and forcibly remove Black people from trains or prevent them from boarding. Second, they would intimidate their families. If one Black family member was leaving, white Southerners would threaten to kick the rest of the family off the property once the train left. Third, they would use legal means. Remember, sharecroppers who owed people money couldn't leave until they paid off the debt. Thus, many landowners drove sharecroppers deeper and deeper into debt. White Southerners also tried to convince potential migrants that it was too cold for them in the North and that since Black people weren't used to cold weather they would starve to death. This wasn't as strong a tactic, because many Black workers responded that they would rather starve to death in Chicago than get lynched in Texas. Since many Black Southerners read about job openings in the North via Black newspapers, white Southerners tried to make it illegal to possess a Black newspaper. Some Southern locales and municipalities outlawed Black newspapers on the grounds of them being incendiary and inciting violence and trouble between the races. White Southerners were so desperate to keep Black labor in the South that often they would send white Southerners up north to try to convince Black people to come back. The white Southerners would lie and say that the Black people would be treated better down South. White Southerners did not just sit by and watch their labor force leave.

When African Americans noticed the efforts that white Southerners were making to keep them in the South, they were confused. White people would lynch them and refuse to let them vote or get a quality education. Black Southerners accepted that white people didn't want them there. Yet white Southerners didn't want them to leave, in direct contradiction to their actions. Despite the best efforts of white Southerners, more than a million Black folks left the South in the first wave. But the Second Great Migration would see more than 3 million people leave the South between 1945 and 1970. The Second Great Migration saw significant numbers of Black people moving to the West Coast: San Francisco, Oakland, Los Angeles, Seattle, and Portland. Seattle is interesting because it was geographically the farthest city but was a desirable location due to jobs at Boeing and McDonnell Douglas. At times when I would travel across the country to conferences, my mom would let me know that we had relatives there. On one occasion I told her that I was going to be in Seattle, and she proceeded to tell me about her cousins who lived there and said if I had time I should go by and see them. It seems like my mom had cousins everywhere, all originally from the small community in Franklinton, Louisiana.

During my last semester teaching at Louisiana State University in the spring of 2007, I noticed an older Black woman sitting in the first row of the lecture hall. She looked like she was in her early sixties. It was the first day of the semester, so after introducing myself I let the class know that my mom was from Franklinton. Within seconds the older woman said, "Are you Cousin Ada's boy?" Ada Warren Burton was my grandma. The woman said, "They told me you were up here." The class was completely shocked. I'm not sure if she knew my mom, my aunts, or my uncles, but it shows how these linkages worked. Whenever I would go to New Orleans or someplace like that, I would say, "Franklinton, Louisiana," and people would just start calling off names. I would say, "I'm from Cleveland," and somebody would say, "Is Peggy Sue your mama?" I'm like, "Yeah! How did you know?" These personal stories are important to me because even though Black Southerners migrated to other parts of the country, they maintained deep connections to their hometowns.

THE PROMISED LAND?

Just like the children of Israel, Black migrants perceived the North as the promised land, a refuge from Pharaoh, or in this case Jim Crow. Yet when they first arrived, they had to deal with criticism from their own community. Middle-class Black folk who had been in some of these cities for decades did not necessarily give their Black brothers and sisters from the South a warm welcome. Middle-class Black folk had concerns that the newcomers didn't know how to act around white people, that they didn't practice good hygiene, and that they were so uncultured that they were disrupting race relations. Some even suggested that Black migrants needed to go to a "finishing school" of some sort. As bad as that was, Black Southern migrants faced considerable opposition outside the Black community. When they arrived in their new locales, Black Southerners didn't find Jim Crow, they found Jim Crow's cousin. As they made the transition to Los Angeles, Chicago, New York, and other places, they had little idea that they would confront unequal schooling, employment discrimination, police brutality, and poor housing.

PUBLIC SCHOOLING

By far the most shocking indignity occurred in the public schools. Although the schools in the North were integrated in theory, most Black migrants found their kids attending all-Black schools. While schools in the South were all-Black or all-white because of de jure segregation, the schools in the North were separate because of de facto segregation: segregation by custom and not by law. Black parents registered a litany of complaints toward public school officials throughout the 1940s, '50s, and '60s. No Black teachers. Severely overcrowded schools. White teachers who didn't know how to connect with Black students. Dilapidated school buildings. Black children being disproportionately placed in LD (learning disability) classes. Black students being disproportionately suspended and disciplined.

The greatest miscarriage of justice occurred because of school overcrowding. In some cities, such as Cleveland, the school system had to send the students to school in shifts: half the school would go in the morning for three and a half hours, and the other half would go in the afternoon for three and a half hours. The question is, How was that possible? How could Ohio, Illinois, New York, or New Jersey allow African American kids to get less than the compulsory six and a half hours of education each day? These school systems applied for a waiver to that rule. This went on in some places for more than five years. The schools were so overcrowded that some kindergarten classes had fifty-one students. Because of de facto school segregation, the schools were overcrowded in Black areas but under capacity in white neighborhoods. As Black students were going to schools in shifts, white schools had half-empty classrooms.

Black parents were also frustrated that there were no Black teachers. People talk a lot about school integration, and textbooks celebrate the *Brown v. Board of Education* Supreme Court decision, but Black parents never wanted their children to be taught by white teachers. Black parents realized that white teachers could not help a Black kid holistically, and many felt that they could not help Black kids academically. The parents were also clear in that they wanted educators who could prepare their children to thrive in a society that was often unwelcoming to them.

JOB DISCRIMINATION

Employment discrimination was also a source of frustration for Black migrants. Although many Black Southerners came north for employment opportunities, they dealt with significant job discrimination when they pursued those jobs, largely because they had to battle vicious stereotypes. Black women dealt with stereotypes that they were mean, had bad attitudes, and were quick to snap back at their superiors. Black men had to deal with the stereotype that they were lazy and incompetent. In many of these factories, although the pay was higher than what they had been earning in the South, they were always given the lowest-paying, most hazardous jobs. They were always subject to the last-hired, first-fired culture when there was an economic downturn. And then they had white coworkers who sometimes did not want to work beside them. If you know anything about labor unions and labor union discrimination, it was well into the '50s and '60s before African Americans were allowed to join the union in some trades.

Black workers also confronted the structural problems of deindustrialization and automation. As Black folk were coming north for factory jobs and making more money, a decline began in the manufacturing industry. Many jobs were replaced with automation, meaning some jobs that had taken ten people to do now could be handled by only one person. Jobs also started moving from the Rust Belt to the Sun Belt. So that was a dynamic of the migration. Black folks were coming for jobs, but jobs were slowly leaving.

Even now employment discrimination is real. Every few years a major publication will present a study of two groups of individuals, one Black and one white, with similar resumes. The only differences are the names of the applicants. Typically, the names of the Black candidates are more distinctively Black, whereas the white candidates will have traditionally white names. On average, white candidates are contacted more often for interviews than Black candidates, if the Black candidates are contacted at all. These studies show that Black applicants with Black-sounding names are discriminated against by not receiving job interviews even though their resumes are similar to, or sometimes better than, those of their white counterparts.

POLICE BRUTALITY

One of the biggest things that divides America is how we view the police. Over the past decade or so, with the systemic police killings of unarmed African Americans, the issue of police brutality has been a popular topic. But Black complaints about unfair police protection are not new. Police brutality has been a fact of life in Black communities since the late 1800s, and as the number of Black people grew in specific Northern cities, there was a parallel rise in police mistreatment. As Black populations grew, white city officials would increase the size of their police forces, but not with local people. They would specifically recruit experienced white police officers from the Deep South. There was a strong belief that white Southerners knew how to handle Negroes. Since these departments were increasingly populated by white Southerners, the departments adopted a hard-line attitude that their number one job was to keep Negroes in line, by any means necessary. Thus, the term "police brutality" is an all-encompassing term. It means aggressive police behavior at one end of the spectrum and outright police murder on the other end. As expected, many of these police departments had very few Black police officers and almost no African American officers in administrative positions. As these inner cities became increasingly Black, hostility increased between Black communities and police departments. What we are seeing now is just a continuation of a larger historical issue.

HOUSING DISCRIMINATION

The key to wealth for most Americans is homeownership, but the real estate industry has long been a place for blatant racial discrimination. As a result it has played a tremendous role in limiting Black family wealth. I'm going to give two personal examples. My wife is from Pasadena, California, a suburb right outside Los Angeles. If you are familiar with college football, you know the Rose Bowl: you can walk there from my in-laws' house.

When my father-in-law moved to Pasadena in the mid-1950s, he and my mother-in-law were steered to the Black section of the city. He was not shown houses in any of the white areas. He was basically told that if he wanted a home in Pasadena, it would be in one particular area. This is a practice called racial steering. It wasn't the law. He could afford a bigger house in a more expensive area, but that option was not available. He settled on Ridgewood Lane and purchased a small, two-bedroom bungalow that was about 1,500 square feet. That house today is worth approximately $785,000 (California real estate is crazy). But if they had been allowed to buy a house literally around the corner in a more exclusive neighborhood, the value of their property would be $1.7 to $3.5 million. That is a considerable difference in wealth.

My parents' situation was similar. They purchased a home in Cleveland Heights, Ohio, in 1963. Our family was one of the first African American families to buy a house in this particular suburb. I remember asking my dad, "When you decided to move to Cleveland Heights, did the realtor show you any other neighborhoods?" He said, "I understood that if we were going to move to Cleveland Heights, they were only going to let me buy a house on one or two streets." These are just two examples, but many African American homeowners can tell similar stories.

When Black folk moved to the North, they were basically steered to all-Black, overcrowded areas, which were characterized by high-density housing, unenforced housing codes, high rents, and communities neglected by white landlords. The overcrowding was so severe that Black migrants lodged wherever possible: basements, garages, makeshift backyard shacks, and places not suitable for residential life, such as abandoned warehouses. They were willing to make these sacrifices because no matter how bad their housing conditions were, they preferred that over living in the South. My mom often shared how disappointed she was when she moved to Cleveland in 1959. She saw Black people living in overcrowded apartments and housing projects, and she couldn't understand how a place like Cleveland, with all that opportunity, or so she thought, had people living in abject poverty.

With continual overcrowding in all-Black areas in the postwar period, local authorities across America decided to invest in public housing as a short-term solution. The "projects," as they have come to be called, quickly became overcrowded, crime-infested, woefully neglected spaces, such that they were not conducive to a healthy quality of life. Some projects, like the Robert Taylor Homes and Pruitt-Igoe, were like miniature cities. Although public housing was initially designed for short-term stays, local authorities soon realized it would become generational for many African American families.

The Great Migration after World War II would forever change the fabric of urban America. While Black people were settling into all-Black ghettos, white homeowners were escaping to the suburbs. This phenomenon is called "white flight," and it has two components: white residential flight and white commercial flight. White people moved to the suburbs, and white-owned businesses left as well. White business owners went to the suburbs in search of more land, lower taxes, and cheaper wages. In a similar vein, white homeowners were drawn to bigger houses, better schools, wide-open parks, and recreational opportunities. The key draw was that the suburbs were all-white.

White flight didn't affect only inner-city neighborhoods and shopping. It changed the landscape of the United States. White flight was not possible without interstate highway construction. The Interstate Highways Act allowed people to move to the suburbs and have an easy commute to the city for work. But even when the highways were being built, there was a racial component. The government rarely built highways through all-white neighborhoods; rather, they would build highways through existing Black neighborhoods and completely change the fabric of these historic Black communities. Black areas were torn apart to make spaces for highways, while white communities were largely unaffected.

When we talk about white people leaving and white flight, understand that in real estate terms, there was something called the tipping point. The tipping point refers to the idea that white people will leave a community once it reaches a certain percentage of Black homeowners. Back in the 1940s, '50s, and '60s, the tipping point was 3 to 5 percent. Some people would even argue that in 2021, the tipping point may be 2 percent. If a neighborhood becomes 2 percent Black, people may start leaving.

Although African Americans are often accused of wanting handouts, many Americans don't realize that the federal government created the white middle class through two very generous federally backed mortgage programs. Prior to the 1940s, if someone wanted to buy a house, they had to have a 20 percent cash down payment. In an effort to populate the suburbs, stimulate the economy, and encourage white homeownership, the government created two loan programs: the Federal Housing Administration (FHA) loan program and the Veterans Administration (VA) loan program. FHA loans allowed prospective white homeowners to acquire a home with just a dollar down. VA loans allowed veterans to purchase a home with just their signature. The federal government was going to back both of those loans. These loan programs were critical for getting white people into homes. Many of the white people who took advantage of these loan programs had never owned a home. These programs allowed the white working class to escape the city, to put their children in better schools, and to build generational wealth through homeownership. In essence, the government gave the white working class the biggest handout possible: a free home.

Unfortunately, the FHA and VA loan programs were off-limits to prospective Black homeowners. Suburban developers, politicians, and white homeowners kept them out through a practice called redlining. Although the FHA and VA loan programs were insured by the federal government, the loans were administered by local banks. Local bank officials were instructed not to provide loans to Black people. In an effort to streamline and simplify the discrimination, bankers would take a map of the city and draw a big red line around Black neighborhoods and their respective zip codes. When African Americans applied for mortgages, the banker would find the address and zip code on the map. If you lived in one of the redlined areas, the loan would be declined regardless of income, credit history, or net worth. One's assets didn't matter because the loan would be denied. Loan officers didn't even have to look at the application. Redlining was a way to keep Black folks not only out of the suburbs but also out of nicer areas within the city.

The second way Black people were kept out of the suburbs was through bans on public transportation. Many suburban areas did not allow public transportation because there was a belief that a subway or bus system would allow low-income (Black) residents to move there. Third, many suburban communities banned apartment buildings and multifamily housing units. Only single-family homes were allowed. Fourth, some suburbs had laws that said no more than two generations of the same family could occupy a dwelling. Although this law made no mention of race, it had a racial intent. African Americans in the North routinely had more than two generations of people living together. The last method used to keep Black people out of the suburbs was a legal document called the "restrictive covenant." Many housing deeds dating back to the 1920s stated explicitly that the property could not be sold to a Negro or to anyone of African descent. Depending upon the location of the home, some deeds would add "Mexican," "Italian," or "Jewish" to the restriction, but "Negro" or "Black" was always listed. The housing deed would prevent the house from being sold to an African American.

White realtors made a lot of money during this period. They used a tactic called blockbusting that exploited the fears of white homeowners while simultaneously exploiting the desires of Black home buyers to leave the inner city. White realtors would pay African American families to go on walking tours of white neighborhoods, pointing out houses that were presumably about to come up for sale. When white homeowners observed that, they would call the realtor and ask, "What's going on?" The realtor would say, "I've got a lot of Negroes looking for homes. They have money and they are going to start moving into your neighborhood. So you better sell while you can, because once they move in, your property values will go down." Out of fear, white homeowners would sell their home at a reduced rate. The white realtor, in turn, would sell the house at a drastically inflated rate to a Black home buyer. Realtors manipulated racial fears to put more money in their pockets.

Race still impacts the housing market today. Let me give the perspective of a Black homeowner. When my wife and I sold our home in Baton Rouge, Louisiana, we had an African American woman as our realtor. Before we put the house on the market, she said, "I need y'all to take down everything Black. Everything. Take your pictures off the wall. Get rid of the Black magazines. Don't let the prospective home buyer know that you are an African American family." Although we were going to "whiten" our house anyway, I was still shocked that we had to do it. The house was just three years old, in a wonderful neighborhood, with a great school system. But the realtor said it didn't matter, because some white home buyers would not want to buy a house that had been previously occupied by an African American family. And guess who ended up buying the house? Another African American family.

Several years after moving to Austin, my wife and I went to visit an African American couple we had met a few weeks prior. When we walked into the house there were pictures of white people and Greek-letter paraphernalia on the walls. I didn't recognize the sorority but I knew it wasn't one of the four Black sororities. I was confused because I knew they were both Black Greeks. I said to the wife, "I thought you were a Delta or AKA and that your husband is a Kappa? What sorority or fraternity is that?" She said, "Leonard, that's a white sorority. We're trying to sell our house and I want them to think we're white."

I read an article in the summer of 2020 about an African American family that had their house appraised as part of the refinancing process. Although the homeowner hadn't wanted to be there when the appraiser arrived, she was. She said the white appraiser appraised their house for about $140,000 less than market value. She hired another appraiser, but this time she made sure that neither she nor her daughter were home. As she expected, the second appraisal was at market value. Real estate discrimination affects multiple aspects of home ownership, even house appraisals.

Black urbanization didn't save Southern Blacks from racism and social injustice. They needed different strategies to combat those issues depending on where they lived. These strategies are reflected in the differing avenues of the civil rights movement.

TEACHING
THE CIVIL RIGHTS
MOVEMENT

I T CAN BE ARGUED THAT THE BLACK FREEDOM struggle started when the first African arrived on the shores of British North America. A more traditional interpretation suggests that the groundwork for what would become the civil rights movement happened during World War II. But there is no official start date. Nobody sent out a tweet that said, "We're going to start the civil rights movement today." The civil rights movement is just a chronology of events where we see a sort of renewed energy on the part of African Americans to demand that the United States live up to the Constitution and grant them their full civil and political rights.

But World War II was a catalyst. More than one million Black soldiers fought during World War II, and when those soldiers got back from overseas, they recognized that although they had fought to make the world safe abroad, they needed support at home. They came home with renewed energy to get Black folks civil rights. A Black newspaper called the *Pittsburgh Courier* launched the Double V campaign, which meant victory at home and victory abroad. Black veterans were becoming aware that they lived a segregated existence in the Unites States, fought in a segregated military with white officers who didn't respect them, helped this country win the war, but couldn't vote or go to a public library when they came back home. As Black soldiers came home, they made a commitment to fight for civil rights by registering to vote (or attempting to do so), joining the National Association for the Advancement of Colored People (NAACP), and leading local movements.

The sight of Black World War II veterans in uniform became a political statement. White Southerners responded with brute force and terror. On several occasions African American veterans were lynched, killed, and brutalized while wearing their uniforms. One of the most horrific cases involved a young man named Isaac Woodard who served in World War II. He was in South Carolina on his way back home, in uniform, and the county sheriff gouged Woodard's eyes out, leaving him permanently blind. White terrorists targeted men and women like Woodard because their military uniforms and unwillingness to accept second-class citizenship were seen as affronts to white supremacy. My dad had to confront this awful reality in 1956. Upon graduating from Case Western Reserve University that year, he had to serve his two years in the military because of the draft. He was sent to Fort McClellan in Anniston, Alabama, where he joined a unit with a large number of Black college graduates. Upon arriving there, they were told to stay on or close to the base and were cautioned to leave the base only on Sunday to go to church. They were also told that under no circumstances were they to leave the base while in their uniform, because they would become targets like Isaac Woodard.

COMBATING SEGREGATION

As Black veterans were confronting Jim Crow, the NAACP continued their legal assault on segregated schooling. In the 1930s and mid-1940s, the NAACP's legal strategy was to integrate professional and graduate schools first, undergraduate education second, and deal with the greatest taboo of them all, K–12 education, last. The University of Texas at Austin played a key role in the NAACP's legal strategy. Established as a university in 1883, UT Austin was able to keep the school all-white because of state law. As long as the state could prove that similar courses of study could be had at all-Black colleges, UT Austin could maintain segregation. This worked at the undergraduate level because the state could point to Prairie View A&M, an HBCU in Prairie View, Texas. Under the separate but equal doctrine, they were technically in compliance with the law. But Prairie View did not have an abundance of graduate programs, nor a single professional school. The state knew they were susceptible to a strong legal challenge from those wanting to attend UT's graduate and professional programs.

As a way to prevent this legal challenge, the state of Texas came up with an out-of-state scholarship program. If you were a Black Texas resident and you wanted to go to graduate or professional school in Texas, the state would provide a scholarship for you to go to school out of state. They did this because they didn't want Black folks to file lawsuits. Instead of participating in lawsuits designed to integrate professional and graduate school education in Texas, many African American students who wanted advanced degrees used the scholarships to attend the University of Michigan, UC-Berkeley, UCLA, Columbia University, Ohio State, and a host of other top-tier universities. As a result, many African Americans received their advanced degrees at more prestigious schools than their white Southern counterparts. Although the state scholarship program worked for a while, some people had no desire to go out of state for an advanced degree. There was much debate in the Black community over whether a lawsuit should be filed to abolish the out-of-state scholarship program.

Heman Sweatt was one such person who did not want to go out of state. The Houston postal worker applied to the University of Texas at Austin School of Law, and he worked with the NAACP to gain admittance. The NAACP filed a lawsuit to integrate the law school in a case known as *Sweatt v. Painter*. Painter was the president of the university at the time. The chances for success were high because there was no Black law school in Texas. In an effort to prevent the UT Law School from integrating, however, the state created the Texas State University for Negroes Law School in the basement of a building behind the state capitol in Austin. Heman Sweatt was to be the only student. Two white professors were assigned to the school, and they purchased about forty books for the makeshift program. This lasted less than a year because it was all a sham. Thurgood Marshall from the NAACP argued convincingly that the newly created law school was not equal in prestige or rigor to the University of Texas Law School. It was far from separate but equal. When the new law school opened in the fall of 1947, UT officials expected literally hundreds of Black students to enroll. Only two students registered, and the school never got off the ground. Texas eventually opened a new HBCU with a law school in Houston, today called Texas Southern University.

Sweatt v. Painter was a precursor to the *Brown v. Board of Education* decision, and it basically outlawed discrimination in graduate and professional school programs. In the fall of 1950, about fifteen Black students enrolled in graduate school at the University of Texas, and Heman Sweatt enrolled in the law school. But he withdrew prior to finishing his first year because of stress and family responsibilities. When the University of Texas integrated its undergraduate programs in 1956 in the aftermath of *Brown*, it was done without conflict. In fact, more than 50 percent of the UT student body wanted the school to integrate. But although integration was without conflict, the university did implement a new component of the admission process: standardized testing. The University of Texas at Austin did not require any form of standardized testing before integration.

When Black people talk about standardized tests being a gatekeeping mechanism, being culturally biased, people often don't believe it. But there is evidence if you look at history. If standardized tests were not needed at the University of Texas until 1956, it's not a coincidence that they were required after integration. They were put in place as a mechanism of control to keep certain people, Black people, out.

While the NAACP's efforts to integrate colleges and universities were met with mild resistance, integrating K–12 education led to a resurgence of white supremacy, and it helped launch the civil rights movement. White fear around school integration had little to do with the educational enterprise; it was squarely based on imagined fears that Black boys would have sexual relations with white girls. White Southerners felt that Black boys would sexually assault white girls, white girls would get pregnant, and this mixing of the races would lead to the eventual decline of the white race. This was not the only reason white Southerners rebelled against integration, but it was a prominent one.

A 1950 survey illustrated white attitudes toward school integration. Seventy-three percent of all whites polled said Black people were less developed intellectually. Seventy percent said Black people were lacking in morality and ambition. Seventy-five percent favored segregation in public education. Another survey asked, "If the schools in your area are integrated, what should be the response?" Some suggested amending the Constitution. Others recommended that their respective states withhold funding from schools that integrated. Predictably, others talked about using violence to prevent change. White moderates agreed to comply with the order and desegregate the schools. But 43 percent of the people polled said that a better solution would be to close all of the schools. They were willing to limit their own children's education if it would prevent school integration. In Virginia and other parts of the South, that's exactly what happened. There is a saying in the Black community: The white man will cut off his arm if it will kill you. Those who suggested closing all schools are a clear illustration of that idea. Ultimately the *Brown* decision outlawed school segregation and it invalidated the 1896 *Plessy v. Ferguson* case that legalized Jim Crow and segregation.

White Southerners responded to the *Brown* decision by creating private schools. If you research private schools in many Southern cities, you will notice a direct correlation between the year the public schools were integrated and the year that a private school was established. Private schools weren't needed during the era of segregation because the schools were already white.

What happened to the public schools and the students who attended them? Once the schools were forced to integrate, white school officials closed Black schools and fired

Black teachers. For example, Franklinton, Louisiana, had one Black and one white elementary, middle, and high school. Logically one would think that some of the white kids would go to the Black school and some of the Black kids would go to the white school. That didn't happen. In many Southern cities, Black high schools completely disappeared.

As Black schools were being closed and white private schools were being opened, Black teachers felt the brunt of the impact. There were fewer jobs now, and the school systems were not going to allow white teachers to lose their jobs because of school integration. Black teachers were fired or moved into different, lesser positions at remaining schools. From 1954 to 1972, forty thousand African American teachers lost their jobs. Now, here's the funny thing, Black teachers knew this was coming. There was even a debate in the Black community about what would happen to the Black educational experience if the schools were integrated. Black teachers warned the community that they would lose their jobs. They also predicted that Black students would suffer from being taught by white teachers, that Black students would no longer have role models in the schools, and that teaching as a profession among Black people would undergo a rapid decline. If you look at the state of Black education in 2021, it is painfully clear how accurate those predictions were.

White backlash wasn't relegated only to schools. When public facilities were integrated, white people adopted an antigovernment, antitaxation ideology. As long as the government preserved segregation—as long as tax money went to whites-only schools, parks, swimming pools, libraries, and other public facilities—white Southerners seldom complained about taxation and big government, because it worked to their benefit. But after the *Brown* decision, Southerners became increasingly antigovernment. They talked about the dangers of big government and government overreach. This attitude is rooted in racism because white Southerners did not want their tax dollars benefiting Black people.

Even now, you can still see some of this antigovernment sentiment even when it works against the interests of the white working class. It's still very popular in Texas, Mississippi, Louisiana, Alabama, and many other Southern states. For example, Beaumont, Texas, sits squarely in the middle of "Cancer Alley," a three-hundred-mile strip of land between New Orleans and Houston that is home to countless chemical plants. On a daily basis these plants pollute the environment, which leads to a disproportionate number of cancer cases. Despite the direct correlation between the chemical plants and bad health outcomes, the white community doesn't want any kind of governmental regulation.

BLACK MONDAY

When the Supreme Court decision in *Brown* was issued on May 17, 1954, that day became Black Monday to white Southerners. It would trigger a visceral and violent response not seen since the Reconstruction period. Mississippi judge Tom Brady documented the ideology of the white response in his book *Black Monday*. This book laid out the massive resistance strategy: he basically said to hell with the Supreme Court case. The government wasn't going to tell white Southerners what to do. They were going to resist by any means necessary. *Black Monday* became the manifesto for white segregationists. Brady provided the justification for massive resistance. He talked about the inevitable sexual relationships between Black men and white women and how that would lead to the mongrelization of society: "Black beasts, rapists will thwart the sanctity of white women." Beyond the scare tactics, the book talked about the restoration of Southern values, which led white Southerners to reimagine their Confederate past. Many white Southerners felt that they were in a second Civil War, so they began to pull out the symbols from the Confederacy. After the *Brown* decision, more Confederate statues were erected, and you began to see the Confederate battle flag. The Confederate battle flag had been relegated to museums before the *Brown* decision.

Black Monday led to the creation of White Citizens' Councils, also known as the "uptown Klan." Every major Southern city had a White Citizens' Council. Unlike the Klan, which was made up of working-class people, council members were typically the city's business and political elite: judges, bankers, business people, principals, school administrators, the very well educated and powerful. Although they were more polished than the Klan, they were unapologetic white supremacists and segregationists. They primarily used economic intimidation, threats of job loss, and violence to keep Black folk from registering to vote and demanding civil rights.

Here is how the White Citizens' Council would operate. If a group of Black people who lived in McComb, Mississippi, went to the courthouse to register to vote, they would not be allowed to register. The registrar would take their names and distribute them to members of the White Citizens' Council. The members of the council would intimidate and threaten the Black citizens. White bosses would threaten to fire Black people, and white landlords would threaten to evict Black people. If you were a Black

business owner, the White Citizens' Council would organize a boycott of your business. There was a lot of economic intimidation. But these citizens' councils were very,
very popular.

One of the expected consequences of the *Brown* decision
was a rise in racial violence and terrorism across the American South. One of the most shocking cases was the lynching of fourteen-year-old Emmett Till, a Chicago native.
During the summer of 1955 he went to Money, Mississippi,
to visit relatives. One afternoon while at a local store,
he allegedly said, "Bye, baby," to the white store owner.
She immediately told her husband about the encounter.
Emmett Till was taken from his uncle's house and lynched
early the next morning. In an effort to show the brutality of white Southerners, his mother, Mamie, decided to
have an open-casket viewing and funeral in Chicago. When
Jet magazine published a photograph of Till's disfigured
corpse, the image was spread across the world. Today it
is one of the most impactful photographs in all of African
American history.

Till was just a fourteen-year-old boy from Chicago, but it
didn't matter. White Southerners felt like their way of life
was under attack, and they needed to send a message. No
one was ever convicted of the Till lynching, and his accuser
recanted her story decades later. The Till lynching inspired
a generation of activists. Similarly, the deaths of George
Floyd and Breonna Taylor in 2020 served to inspire a new
generation of activists. But this is not unique; throughout much of the Black freedom struggle, whenever there
was a violent death, Black activists would press for more
social change.

The Till lynching triggered a renewed spirit of African American activism, but it also convinced some Black

Northerners to never go to the South. My dad—born in Indianapolis and raised in Cleveland, Ohio—said he never planned to go to the South after seeing that image. My father-in-law had similar sentiments. He was born in Many, Louisiana, but went to Oklahoma and then to Chowchilla, California, in the 1930s with his parents and siblings. He often said that he had no desire to go back to where he was born.

As white Southerners embraced racial violence, a debate emerged in the Black community around armed self-defense. Robert Williams, a military veteran from Monroe, North Carolina, and president of the Monroe NAACP, and his wife, Mabel Williams, would be the strongest advocates for this approach in the late 1950s. Robert Williams stated that Black people were "going to meet violence with violence. We're going to defend ourselves." In essence he was advocating for Black people's Second Amendment rights. They weren't going to let people get brutalized and shot anymore. The middle-class Black folks in Monroe left the NAACP over this rhetoric. Williams rebuilt the chapter by reaching out to the Black working class, folks who were downtrodden and didn't have much education. He was successful in keeping Black people safe from white terrorism in Monroe; however, his approach led the conservative NAACP to suspend him from the organization. Understand, Robert Williams and others weren't talking about going into white neighborhoods and shooting people or burning houses. But it was controversial because nobody had ever heard Black people talk about meeting violence with violence. Similarly, Black people in Bogalusa, Louisiana, just twenty miles from my mother's hometown of Franklinton, embraced armed self-defense as well by organizing the Deacons for Defense and Justice.

Proponents of armed self-defense such as Williams would argue that the Second Amendment did not just give rights to white people; it applied to Black people as well. During the racial disturbances of 2020, there were many instances where it appeared that the Second Amendment only applied to white people. At one particular demonstration at the Michigan State Capitol, an armed, predominantly white group stood outside the capitol as if they were a militia. They all had rifles, what appeared to be AR-15s, over their shoulders. And there was no kind of police repression at all. Contrast this with some of the repression tactics we see used against unarmed Black protestors. The question becomes, What would happen if Black folks had a protest at the Texas State Capitol where they were exercising their Second Amendment rights? I'd argue, it wouldn't be tolerated. In all of these debates about the Second Amendment, there's this fundamental question: Who does it apply to?

THE MONTGOMERY BUS BOYCOTT

The Montgomery Bus Boycott of 1955 to 1956 was, more than anything else, an economic movement. The 381-day protest would introduce the world to an activist named Rosa Parks, a Montgomery organization called the Women's Political Council, and a young pastor named Martin Luther King Jr. The boycott was impactful because public buses were one of the only places where Blacks and whites were certain to interact on a daily basis. Although the vast majority of all bus revenues in Montgomery came from Black passengers, they dealt with a variety of abuses on their daily commutes. First, they had to pay their fare at the front of the bus, get off, and walk to the back to board. On many occasions the bus would speed off. Second, bus drivers would assault Black passengers verbally and physically. Considering that many bus drivers were armed, these insults could turn violent rather quickly. Third, the buses had a movable sign that dictated where whites sat (in front of the sign) and where Black people sat (behind the sign). In some situations, Black people had to stand in the rear of the bus while the white section of the bus was completely empty. Last, many of the bus stops in Black neighborhoods were a great distance apart, but the bus stops in white neighborhoods were at almost every block.

What makes this even more problematic is that 70 to 80 percent of the bus revenues in Montgomery came from Black passengers. They were the economic engine behind the bus company, and the Black community was fed up with dealing with the injustices. The Women's Political Council of Montgomery decided to launch a boycott when Claudette Colvin, a teenager, was brutalized on the bus and arrested. But they didn't want Claudette to be the symbol of the boycott, because she was pregnant. This was a matter of respectability. They understood that if they launched a boycott, people wouldn't follow it, because Claudette wouldn't be seen as respectable enough to American society. But when Rosa Parks, a longtime activist in her own right, refused to give up her seat to a white man, the boycott began and she became a national symbol.

Black women did much of the work behind the scenes during the thirteen-month boycott, but the media chose to focus on the spokesperson of the movement, Martin Luther King Jr. Dr. King had just arrived in Montgomery to pastor the influential Dexter Avenue Baptist Church. Because of the inherent chauvinism in movement politics, the Women's Political Council knew that a Black male needed to be the face of the movement. King became the spokesperson, but he never took credit; he would always give credit to the Women's Political Council in Montgomery, Alabama. The Women's Political Council and the Montgomery Improvement Association agreed to let King become the spokesperson for three reasons. One, he was new to the city and he didn't have any enemies, Black or white. Two, he pastored a very influential church. Three, he had the ability to connect with people from all walks of life. King could talk to well-educated as well as uneducated Black folks and make all of them feel valued. Despite King's popularity, he was not the leader of the boycott. Black women were. They were the organizers and provided much of the inspiration needed to sustain the boycott.

I didn't realize the significance of the Montgomery Bus Boycott until I went to Jackson State University, in Jackson, Mississippi. During my freshman year, my friend from Milwaukee and I went to Metrocenter Mall and stayed until the mall closed at 9:00 p.m. We headed to the bus stop, and before we realized it, we had been standing there for more than an hour. Eventually a security guard came out and I asked, "Do you know what time the next bus comes?" And he said, "The buses stop running at five." This was the fall of 1989, when the buses stopped running in Jackson, Mississippi, at 5:00 p.m. When I got back to class the next week I asked my professor why the buses stopped so early. He told me something so profound. In the South, the bus system was created for one kind of Black person, for one purpose: to take Black domestics to and from white homes and nothing else. There was no need for them to be on the bus after 5:00 p.m. I also learned that in the South white people didn't ride the bus. That explained why the bus company in Montgomery was dependent upon Black passengers.

MOBILIZER VERSUS ORGANIZER

When we talk about the civil rights movement, there is a need to distinguish between a mobilizer and an organizer. King was a mobilizer. He showed up to a city where people were mobilizing for action. But organizers are more important than mobilizers. Here's why. An organizer is someone doing the day-to-day work, dealing with grassroots folks behind the scenes. They rarely get any attention, but their tireless work raises the political consciousness of a people. When it is time to boycott, protest, march, or demonstrate, the people can be easily activated. Throughout the movement, Black women were doing the organizing, and many of them had been radicalized through domestic work because they had direct contact with white people on a daily basis.

Martin Luther King Jr.'s mentor, Ella Baker, was a powerful organizer. Throughout much of the 1930s, the North Carolina native traveled throughout the South establishing NAACP branches. Her tireless work behind the scenes was characterized by getting to know people, building relationships, speaking in churches and family rooms, and encouraging people to get engaged in the Black freedom struggle. If anybody was singlehandedly responsible for the growth of NAACP membership in the South in the '30s, '40s, and '50s, it was Ella Baker. She was acquainted with the more popular Thurgood Marshall, but in many ways she became the face of the NAACP because she was doing the work. In the 1940s she took on a national role with the NAACP as director of branches. In 1952 she became president of the New York NAACP. And in 1957 Martin Luther King Jr. reached out to her. He was starting a new organization and needed her help.

Although King and Baker had a close relationship, there

was tension between them. Baker did not like the idea of leaders being placed on a pedestal or above the people they were serving. She didn't like hierarchical leadership. One of her most famous quotes is, "Strong people don't need strong leaders." She also grew frustrated at the male dominance of the movement, and she made it clear that much of its success could be traced to the day-to-day work of Black women activists. Baker's work with King was critical because she was one of the few people whose mentorship he accepted. She used that respect to shape his career, to give him direction, and to tell him what he needed to hear.

Another seldom-mentioned organizer was Septima Clark. She operated the Highlander Folk School in Tennessee in the 1950s and 1960s, where she taught Black people how to read and write, how to register to vote and participate in the political process, and about participatory democracy. The Highlander Folk School trained a generation of activists, including Rosa Parks, who visited the school a year before the Montgomery Bus Boycott. As the lives of Baker and Clark illustrate, Black women were instrumental in the movement. It can be argued that without the tireless work of women like Baker and Clark, the movement might not have existed.

While the groundwork for the civil rights movement was being laid, the United States was engaged in a Cold War with Russia. Civil rights activists would use the rhetoric of the Cold War to embarrass America on the world stage. As a communist nation, Russia argued that its economic and political system was drastically superior to capitalism and democracy. When the United States asserted that democracy was the best form of government, Russia would call out the treatment of African Americans and accuse the United States of being hypocritical. As a result of this global tension, civil rights activists often deliberately provoked white law enforcement officers in an effort to trigger a violent response—so that they could display America's racism across the world.

THE SIT-IN MOVEMENT

Although sit-in protest tactics had been used as early as the 1940s, the sit-in movement that was launched in 1960 by a group of students at North Carolina A&T University ushered in a new generation of college student activism. Students at the historically Black college in Greensboro, North Carolina, pioneered the tactic of going into the whites-only section of an establishment—restaurant, bus or train depot, library—and demanding service. If the service was not provided, they would "sit in" until they were served. They would even show up at a segregated swimming pool and jump in the water. There was shock value to sit-ins. White patrons and business owners were horrified at the blatant disregard for Jim Crow rules. It was a largely successful tactic, however, because many white business owners eventually decided to integrate rather than have constant interruptions at their place of business. Now here's something to consider: What was the response from Black business owners? Some owners perhaps got offended because of the perception that their services were not good enough for their community. Malcolm X, who I will cover in more detail in the next chapter, often talked about how puzzling the sit-in movement was. He would argue that if the white man didn't want to serve you, why would you trust him to make the food? Malcolm was critical of this approach and he attributed it to the Black idea that "the white man's ice is colder." If it was a white-owned restaurant, bakery, or dry cleaner, then somehow it had to be better than what we had in the Black community. Despite Malcolm's critique, the sit-ins were designed to shock white Southerners, to trigger a confrontation, and to get laws changed.

While things like boycotting buses, registering people to vote, and sitting in seem rather conservative by today's standards, these were truly radical efforts because they were direct threats to white supremacy. I often laugh when I hear people criticizing Al Sharpton, Jesse Jackson, and Black Lives Matter activists in one breath and talking about the virtuous tactics of Martin Luther King Jr. in another breath. People often criticize Sharpton and Jackson for seeking headlines and organizing protests. But King functioned very much the same way between the time of the Montgomery Bus Boycott and his death in 1968. Why? Because he was a mobilizer. It was his responsibility to raise awareness around racial injustice. I often remind students that King was not fully embraced as an American hero until his death. Much of white America didn't like him, and plenty of Black folk disliked him as well because he was "messing stuff up." Now people embrace King; it's the King of 1963, however, and not of 1968. America wants the "I Have a Dream" King. That version is safe and palatable. Most people imagine a world where people are judged by the content of their character and not the color of their skin. This dream is in stark contrast to the King of 1968, who would remark, "America has given the Black man a bounced check and now it is time to pay up." Because we have allowed people to distort his message, even the most die-hard opponents of civil rights and Black progress are always quick to invoke the name of King in a "what would Martin Luther King think" fashion.

CIVIL RIGHTS ORGANIZATIONS

Securing voting rights and abolishing segregation were the two goals of the civil rights movement. These goals were clear, transparent, and visible to all. In an effort to chip away at Jim Crow, a host of organizations and individuals emerged to attack these twin evils. This is important to understand because much of the criticism toward the Black Lives Matter movement is that people are unclear on BLM's goals and aims, although they are clearly listed on the website. Nonetheless, the goals of BLM are somewhat more complex and nuanced; this simply was not the case during the civil rights movement. With such stark legal fixtures as segregation, the civil rights movement articulated specific goals addressed at dismantling these explicit policies of discrimination.

By 1960 there were four prominent national civil rights organizations. The NAACP was still the most popular, and their strategy had not changed: they wanted to bring about racial justice through the court system. The Congress of Racial Equality (CORE) believed in direct action, and they reintroduced a strategy called the freedom rides: Black and white citizens would get on buses in Northern cities, and as they traveled through the South they would refuse to move to the back of the bus or to sit in segregated waiting rooms. The third organization was the Southern Christian Leadership Conference (SCLC), established by King and largely made up of pastors. Lastly, the Student Nonviolent Coordinating Committee (SNCC, pronounced "SNICK") was an organization largely made up of Black and white college students. King initially tried to organize college activists under the SCLC banner, but Ella Baker told the students that they would be more effective if they created a separate organization.

These national organizations all had local chapters. Between 1960 and 1965 they would launch campaigns in local cities designed to raise awareness and political consciousness around the issues of segregation and disenfranchisement. One of the first such campaigns was launched in 1961 by SNCC in Albany, Georgia. SNCC launched a variety of protest activities with the goal of forcing the city to integrate. In an effort to disrupt SNCC, Albany's political and economic elite invited King and the SCLC to Albany to help them work out a compromise. To the dismay of SNCC, King accepted the invitation and basically co-opted the SNCC-led movement. Despite his best efforts at getting the city of Albany to work in good faith, King and the SCLC were ultimately unsuccessful in desegregating the city. This tension in Albany illustrated the generational divide that would at times be present during the movement. Additionally, King's involvement in Albany caused some Black observers to suggest that he was just chasing headlines and not really interested in building strong local movements.

The years 1961 and 1962 reintroduced America to the freedom rides, a protest designed to integrate interstate travel. Public interstate bus or train travel was a challenge for African American travelers. Although the Supreme Court's *Boynton v. Virginia* decision had outlawed racial segregation in bus terminals for routes that crossed state lines, the law was not enforced. Upon arriving at bus stations in the South, freedom riders would attempt to integrate restaurants and waiting rooms. The freedom rides were strategic in that they were designed to provoke a violent response from white segregationists, which would then force politicians to act. White supremacists firebombed a bus carrying freedom riders outside of Anniston, Alabama (where my dad was stationed years earlier), and another set of freedom riders was brutally beaten upon arriving in Birmingham, Alabama. The strategy worked. In the summer of 1961 President John F. Kennedy ordered the Interstate Commerce Commission to enforce the law requiring integration in interstate transportation.

Fresh on the heels of the Albany debacle, Martin Luther King Jr. and the Southern Christian Leadership Conference decided to join a local campaign in Birmingham, Alabama, a ruthless city with a deep legacy of white supremacy. When King launched his campaign, however, he was opposed both by white supremacists and segregationists and by the Black elite and Black pastors. One of the biggest myths about the civil rights movement is that it was birthed or rooted in the Black church. That is only partially true. Spiritually, it was rooted in the Black church, but many African American pastors did not eagerly embrace movement activity until they were forced to out of shame. They said King was moving too fast; they called him a radical; they told him that things would get better; and they basically told him that they didn't need him coming to Birmingham stirring up trouble. (Ironically, many of the criticisms hurled toward Black Lives Matter activists in the summer of 2020 were the same accusations and critiques that were leveled at King in 1963.) Despite the opposition, the Alabama Christian Movement for Human Rights welcomed King and the SCLC.

One of the primary reasons the SCLC chose Birmingham, in addition to the city's unwavering commitment to white supremacy, was because it had a public safety commissioner named Bull Connor who had no reservations about using violence to enforce segregation. SCLC leadership and King understood that Bull Connor could not control himself and that he would be very easy to provoke.

Through provocation, they were hoping to trigger a violent response, and they did. Throughout the demonstrations in Birmingham in the spring of 1963, activists faced water hoses, German shepherds, and outright terrorism. These images are so deeply woven into the fabric of American culture that in many ways they symbolize the entire Black freedom struggle. Two months after the Birmingham campaign ended, local members of the Ku Klux Klan bombed the Sixteenth Street Baptist Church on a Sunday morning, claiming the lives of four little girls. Hours later two African American boys were shot and killed in other parts of the city, one by a white police officer and the other by white teenagers. Although the racial violence of the Birmingham campaign would eventually play a role in the passage of the 1964 Civil Rights Act, it was not necessarily successful in ending segregation in Birmingham. In a controversial move, King called off the Birmingham protests after city officials agreed to integrate restrooms and water fountains, to accept a plan to desegregate lunch counters, to improve Black employment, to release jailed protestors, and to establish a biracial human rights commission.

In 1964 SNCC would launch Freedom Summer, the most ambitious attack upon segregation and disenfranchisement. It was an all-out assault on the entire state of Mississippi in an effort to bring Jim Crow to its knees. That summer SNCC sent Black and white college students from the North to Mississippi with two goals: register Black people to vote and establish freedom schools for young people. They wanted to launch freedom schools because Black kids in Mississippi were not getting a quality education in the traditional school year. During a summer experience, these kids could learn things that they should have been learning from August to May.

If there was one person who embodied the spirit of Mississippi and Freedom Summer, it was Mrs. Fannie Lou Hamer. She lived and worked on a plantation in rural Sunflower County until she was forty-four years of age, and she became radicalized when the young activists of SNCC encouraged her to vote. After an unsuccessful attempt to register in Indianola, Mississippi, she was kicked off the plantation and she relocated to nearby Tallahatchie County.

Like many Black Mississippians, Fannie Lou Hamer had a lot to be upset about. She had experiences that were very typical for a lot of Black women in Mississippi. In 1961 she was given what they called a "Mississippi appendectomy." She went to the hospital for a routine procedure, but they gave her a hysterectomy without her permission. It was very common in Mississippi, Alabama, Louisiana, and other parts of the South to forcibly sterilize Black women, because there was this idea that Black people were a drain on taxpayers. So oftentimes a Black woman would go for a normal checkup or a routine procedure, only to be given a hysterectomy. And that is an aspect of history that many historians are just beginning to uncover.

Once Fannie Lou Hamer got involved with SNCC, she became a mentor to many of the students. They were drawn to her because of her authenticity. She was a country girl. She was what we call "down-home." She had a very dynamic spirit and she had the unique ability to connect with people in the field as well as people who claimed to be important. Another thing the people in SNCC liked about Fannie Lou Hamer was that she was a walking testament to Black courage. When she told her story about living on a plantation for forty-four years with her husband and her younger relatives, people could relate to that. She talked about being a timekeeper on the Marlow plantation and how that gave her leadership ability because she had to connect with everybody. Because of her age and stature in the community, she was also able to connect with people of her generation. Although she had very little education, the passion and cadence in her voice allowed her to speak life into people. She represented the best of what Black Mississippi had to offer.

Freedom Summer consisted of SNCC activists going into the Mississippi Delta and building relationships with people. One of the things I tell activists nowadays—and I don't claim to be an activist at all, I just teach Black history—is that too often activists want to impose upon people what they think they need. People need to ask the community if it's okay for them to come, how they can help, and how they can use whatever privilege and clout they have to get initiatives handled. What I love about SNCC is that they understood the value of building relationships with people.

In June 1964 three SNCC activists, one Black and two white, were murdered outside Philadelphia, Mississippi. Andrew Goodman and Mickey Schwerner, the white activists, were from New York. James Chaney was a native Mississippian. Their deaths became an international story, not necessarily because they were civil rights workers but because two of the three were white and from the North. The deaths of Schwerner, Goodman, and Chaney became the violent incident needed to secure passage of the 1964 Civil Rights Act, which outlawed segregation and any other discrimination based on race. Something to ponder, however, is why it took a violent death or violent deaths for legislation to get passed.

With the passage of the 1964 Civil Rights Act, the movement now wanted to use the momentum to draw attention to the lack of voting rights. Civil rights organizations converged on Alabama in March 1965 and planned a march from Selma to the state capitol in Montgomery. On the day of the march, Black and white protestors were brutally attacked by white officers on horseback, beaten with clubs, and tear gassed. This horrific event is now referred to as Bloody Sunday. Once these images were broadcast across the globe, President Lyndon Baines Johnson had the support needed to get the Voting Rights Act of 1965 passed. This legislation placed the federal government in charge of all elections and it outlawed discriminatory voting practices. When LBJ signed the legislation in 1965, it was said that he remarked, "We've just lost the white Southern vote for the next generation." LBJ understood that signing that legislation as a Democrat meant that white Southerners would leave the Democratic Party for the Republican Party. They felt as if their rights as white Southerners had been sold out by one of their own, a white Southern president. Now that Black Southerners had gotten the right to vote, the movement shifted to the nation's urban areas, where the tactics and strategies would be completely different.

TEACHING
BLACK POWER

THE BLACK FREEDOM STRUGGLE UNDERWENT A massive shift in the summer of 1965, when the Watts area of Los Angeles erupted with four days of racial protests. Whites were shocked that this happened in Los Angeles because they were largely unaware of Black dissatisfaction outside of the South. Quite frankly, even in places outside the South, Black and white people were living in two separate worlds. White newspapers did not cover Black news, let alone Black frustration. If you read the *Los Angeles Times* and then the *Los Angeles Sentinel*, the city's Black paper, you would think they were covering two entirely different cities. The riots lasted four days, claimed thirty-four lives, and caused over $40 million in property damage. White Americans didn't have any idea there was this much anger among Black people living outside the segregated South, since there were no visible barriers of discrimination. But there was tons of racial resentment. Virtually every major Northern city would have racial disturbances because Black complaints were

largely ignored by those in power. Many of these grievances went back decades.

Now, I don't like the term "riot" per se, because it is
often used only in reference to Black people. How about
we use the term "political protest"? This form of political
protest was different from the typical racial disturbance
in that up until 1965, the typical race "riot" had involved
white people going into Black neighborhoods and assault-
ing and killing innocent Black civilians. In the 1965 disturbance, African American people were largely taking out
their anger in their own neighborhood by burning down
white-owned property. In the aftermath of the George
Floyd killing, some of the political protests that occurred
in Minneapolis were similar. Many observers asked, "Why
are people burning down their own community?" This is a
fair question. But typically many of the businesses in low-
income communities aren't owned by people who live in
the neighborhood. People were saying that several months
ago, and they were saying it back in the 1960s. Watts
shifted the nation's attention from civil rights activity in
the South to the intractable, structural issues within inner-
city America, such as poor housing, unequal schooling, high
unemployment, and police brutality in large urban areas.

While Black people in the urban areas outside the South
appreciated the four major civil rights organizations—
NAACP, SCLC, CORE, and SNCC—they realized that the
tactics used in the South to secure integration and voting
rights would not work in their communities. A message
of nonviolent massive resistance would fall on deaf ears
because in theory there were no racial barriers. The one
organization that would emerge by the mid-1950s to articulate the frustration of the Black masses outside the South
was the Nation of Islam.

THE NATION OF ISLAM

Most people are aware of the Nation of Islam because of Malcolm X. Let me be clear, Malcolm X never led the Nation of Islam. His official title was national spokesperson. Established in Detroit in the 1930s, the Nation (as it is often called) is not traditional Islam. The theology of the Nation is a mixture of traditional Islam, the Bible, the teachings of Marcus Garvey, Freemasonry, and the teachings of Noble Drew Ali. In essence, the Nation developed a belief system to meet the unique needs of Black people in America.

For those of us who follow a different faith tradition, the Nation's theology can be confusing. The core doctrine of the Nation of Islam is that the white man is the devil and the Black man is God. Portraying the white man as the devil helped Black people in America understand or make sense of their unique situation. Members of the Nation would often talk about the unearned suffering of Black people: "What did Black people do in America for white people to treat us like this?" Portraying the Black man as God gave African Americans the belief that their situation can be changed, that they are in control of that change because they are close to the divine. So you've got this core doctrine: the white man is the devil and the Black man is God. Now, in terms of a theology, the Nation of Islam taught that the Black man was the original man and that white people were the product of a mad scientist who took Black genes and created a completely new race of people characterized by pale skin, thin blood, and small brains. But over time the white man was able to control and dominate the Black nation through tricknology: tricks, lies, and deception. The white man then took the original people (Black people) from Africa and Asia and brought them to the wilderness of North America. When they got to the United States the white man killed the first generation of Black people, so that the original people would be completely cut off from their religion, culture, and customs. Without anyone to teach them about their history, the original people looked to the enslaver for an identity.

This historical interpretation helped the Nation explain the downtrodden condition of Black America. Since the original people were cut off from any knowledge of themselves, they soon got caught up in a host of social ills: crime, drugs, alcohol, sex outside of marriage, mistreatment of women, unemployment, welfare, and unrighteous living. If the first generation of Black folk were killed off, the second, third, and subsequent generations had nowhere to go to understand how to live.

But the Nation offered three ways that the so-called Negroes could get back to the ways of the original people. First, you had to give up the white man's name. When adults joined the Nation, they were encouraged to change their name to an Arabic name, such as Muhammad, Shabazz, or Ali. For those who did not wish to adopt an Arabic name, they were encouraged to use an X, which symbolized the unknown names of Black people that were stolen in slavery. For example, if I were to join the Nation of Islam mosque in Cleveland in 1962 and I wanted an X, they might say, "OK, your name is now Leonard 4X." That would mean that I was the fourth Leonard to join that particular mosque. To reiterate, the X signifies that I don't know my original name because it was stolen during slavery and a European name was imposed upon me.

Second, members of the Nation characterized Christianity as the white man's religion and arguably the preeminent vehicle for brainwashing. They wanted converts to understand that Islam was the Black man's religion and that Christianity was a religion imposed upon them by the enslaver as a mechanism of control. The Nation knew that it would not be easy to separate people from the Black church. To that end the typical Nation of Islam mosque held Sunday services in the afternoon so they would not compete with traditional Black churches. They understood that until someone was truly converted, they would probably go to a traditional Black church in the morning and then come to the mosque in the afternoon.

Last, a convert had to stay physically fit and be properly nourished. The Nation had strict dietary laws that were designed to ensure good health and a long life. They argued that many of the eating habits of Black people were products of life on the white man's plantation. Pork, chitterlings, and other soul food staples were off-limits to converts. As the name implies, the Nation considered themselves just that, a separate nation, and their dietary laws were structured not only to provide them with a healthier life but also to distinguish them from outsiders.

The Nation of Islam believed in traditional gender roles. They taught that since the Black man was God, the Black woman's role was to support the Black man. Many outsiders considered the Nation's teachings offensive to women. Women had to dress modestly, were not allowed to talk to men other than their husbands, and were taught that the highest role of a woman was in the home. Women joined the Nation because it gave them a sense of identity and it gave them protection. They understood that if they were harassed on the street, the men of the Nation would exact retribution on their harasser. They also felt that Black women within the Nation of Islam were celebrated, while Black women outside the Nation were disrespected.

So they didn't see themselves as being oppressed. They saw themselves as one piece of a larger puzzle trying to resurrect the Black nation.

In elementary school one of my best friends, Ferrell, and his family converted to the Nation of Islam. One day after school he told me that he had a new name. "My parents changed my name to Sharrieff, and my last name is Saleem," he said. I don't remember asking why. It wasn't until years later that I realized they were members of the Nation of Islam. By chance, in the late 1980s, Cleveland's Nation of Islam mosque relocated to just down the street from my parents' house.

MALCOLM X AND THE NATION OF ISLAM

Despite the Nation's existence dating back to the 1930s, it did not become popular until Minister Malcolm X became its national spokesperson, and he quickly came to embody the best about the organization. Malcolm, like many converts to the Nation, had some trauma early in his life. His dad was murdered and his mom later suffered a nervous breakdown and was sent to a state hospital. He and his siblings were separated and placed in foster care and the care of relatives. During his teenage years and into his twenties he turned to crime, which landed him in prison. In prison he would be exposed to the teachings of Elijah Muhammad and the Nation of Islam, and at the urging of his brother he became a convert. While in prison Malcolm turned his jail cell into a college classroom, and he transitioned into an organic intellectual. After his prison term Malcolm traveled the country on behalf of Elijah Muhammad, and he singlehandedly established between thirty and forty mosques. In the process he launched *Muhammad Speaks*, the first newspaper of the Nation of Islam.

Malcolm was unique in that he was both an organizer and a mobilizer. He spent time going across the country, building relationships, starting mosques, and spreading the teachings of Elijah Muhammad and the Nation of Islam. He could mobilize both Muslims and non-Muslims with his charisma, his intellect, his stinging critiques of America, and his haranguing critiques about the civil rights movement. To begin with, he felt that the whole premise of the civil rights movement was based on the idea that white people would accept Black folks; he believed that white folks would never accept Black people. Second, he was also critical of the civil rights movement because he said it made Black people become beggars. He said, Why would you try to integrate a white-owned restaurant when you could own your own? His third critique was based on the idea that the civil rights movement did not offer a fundamental critique of US society. He said the movement was based on a romantic notion that this country was actually built for all people. And fourth, he did not believe in the strategy of nonviolence. He felt that the strategy made Black people weak and that it got many innocent Black women and children killed because Black men were unwilling to fight back.

Despite Malcolm being instrumental in the growth and development of the Nation of Islam, he left the organization after a disagreement over tactics with his mentor and savior, Elijah Muhammad. Malcolm wanted the Nation to be much more engaged in the civil rights battles of the South, but Elijah Muhammad preferred for the Nation to stay out of mass protests, since they didn't believe in integration. Malcolm earned a suspension from the Nation in the aftermath of John F. Kennedy's assassination. When asked by a reporter what he thought of Kennedy's death,

Malcolm replied that it was a case of the chickens coming home to roost. During his indefinite suspension Malcolm learned that Elijah Muhammad had fathered countless children with young women and girls in the Nation. Completely distraught, Malcolm left the Nation for good.

In 1964, Malcolm X went to Mecca and underwent a spiritual transformation; he saw Muslims of all shades and colors and he renounced his affiliation with the Nation of Islam in favor of traditional Islamic beliefs. After returning to the United States, and shortly before he was assassinated in February 1965, he changed his name to El-Hajj Malik El-Shabazz. Malcolm's impact on Black history and culture is immeasurable.

When students compare Malcolm and MLK, I have to remind them that they operated in two different worlds. Malcolm X was a Northerner. He was going to talk loud. He was going to be a little bit more courageous because he had more freedoms in his life. King, operating out of the segregated South and coming from the Black church, was more conservative. King's message worked in the South, but when King tried to launch an open housing campaign in Chicago in 1966, it failed miserably. Similarly, Malcolm X's message worked in Harlem, Brooklyn, Detroit, Chicago, Cleveland, Los Angeles, and other cities, but it did not resonate with many Black Southerners. They were operating in two different spheres. Ironically, at times when King was trying to get legislation passed, he would challenge leaders and say, "Now, you got two choices. You can deal with me, or you can deal with Brother Malcolm and them who are outside." Given the choice, many white leaders chose MLK. Regardless of their tactics, Malcolm X and Martin Luther King Jr. were products of their environment, and they spoke to, in many ways, their respective constituents.

THE BLACK PANTHER PARTY

If you ask most Americans what comes to mind when they think of the Black Panther Party you will get a similar answer: Black men in berets and leather jackets walking around with guns threatening white people. While some of this is true, I believe that the Black Panther Party is one of the most misunderstood organizations in all of American history.

Established by Huey Newton and Bobby Seale in Oakland, California, in 1966, the Panthers were an outgrowth of a Black student group at Merritt College that placed more emphasis on community uplift than campus transformation. Founded on the idea of taking it to the streets, the Black Panthers initially were formed with the goal of combating police brutality. Within the first year, the Panthers would have several highly publicized confrontations with police that catapulted them into the national media spotlight. This media attention led to the establishment of Panther chapters throughout America and in other parts of the African diaspora. The Panthers had police patrols where members followed police officers and observed their interactions with Black people. The Panthers would walk with weapons, talking about their constitutional right to bear arms and speaking boldly about defending their community from rogue cops. They believed in armed self-defense and in policing the police.

While police patrols were a direct response to a community need, the Panthers also confronted the police because they believed cops were the most visible agents of capitalist oppression. Politically, the Black Panther Party defined itself as a revolutionary Black nationalist organization, and they wanted a socialist overthrow of America. Although the Panthers attacked racism and racist institutions, they didn't consider white racism to be America's greatest problem. In their eyes capitalism was America's greatest evil.

Although many people associate the Black Panther Party with police confrontations, they created a range of survival programs to meet the needs of poor Black people on a daily basis. Their most popular program was called Free Breakfast for Children. Upon realizing that a lot of inner-city kids went to school hungry, they created a program to provide breakfast for the children. Other projects included a visiting physicians' clinic, a free ambulance program, sickle cell anemia awareness, liberation schools, and a bus service providing transportation to visit loved ones in prison. These programs served several purposes. Number one, they met the practical needs of people in the community. Number two, they were a recruiting mechanism. The presence of politically active and engaged young people was extremely attractive to those who wanted to uplift their community. Last, they were a way to generate money for the organization. Although some in the Black community disagreed with the Panthers' tactics, they could not disagree with the range of services they were offering poor inner-city residents for free.

In addition to meeting community needs, the Panthers also had strong ideas about resurrecting Black manhood. Despite the rank-and-file membership of the Party being overwhelmingly female, Panther leadership was overwhelmingly male. They believed in resurrecting the Black male image to counter the narrative of Black men being weak. They argued that the civil rights movement further damaged the image of Black men because it portrayed them as weak, timid, scared, and cowardly. When you see them in berets and leather jackets or with guns, they are trying to portray a more masculine image of Black men.

Despite being committed members of the Black Panther Party, Black women had to confront the sexist attitudes of men within the organization. Privately, female Panthers would talk about the insecurity of Black men and how the women had to delicately maneuver so that the men's egos weren't damaged. Nonetheless, Black women in the party often confronted sexist attitudes that resulted in verbal abuse, harassment, and assaults. The militaristic leadership structure of the party played a major role in creating this environment. For example, in many chapters party members were assigned specific ranks, and women would talk about men in superior positions using their rank for sexual favors. Women in the party understood that sexism existed, but like many activist women, they made a strategic decision to first fight racism before fighting sexism. They did this because many Black women in the party identified as Black first. The Black Panther Party did not function without women, and they could be found holding a variety of leadership positions at the local and national levels. Although Black men in the party got the headlines, Black women were present on police patrols, led demonstrations, and directed and operated the party's survival programs. While we know many of their names, such as Assata Shakur, Elaine Brown, Ericka Huggins, and Angela Davis, there are countless others who worked in obscurity for the love of their people.

During my time at LSU I started a church for college students and we invited Afeni Shakur, Tupac's mother, to come speak. It was either 2005 or 2006. Over four hundred college students and community members attended. Although she talked mostly about her son's legacy, some audience members asked her about her time in the Black

Panthers. I remember her words vividly. "Leave that Black Panther shit on the wall and in a frame because although the organization did a ton of good it also did a ton of bad." I believe she was specifically referring to the way women were treated in the party.

BLACK POWER AND HIGHER EDUCATION

The Black Panther Party and the Nation of Islam represented two Black Power organizations, but the spirit of Black Power would affect almost every institution in American culture—none more so than higher education. Although the majority of Black college students in America during the mid-1960s were still attending historically Black colleges and universities (HBCUs), the Black students at predominantly white institutions (PWIs) wanted to make these institutions more responsive to their needs. Many institutions typically took proactive steps, particularly after MLK's assassination, to get more Black students to the campus.

PWIs created outreach programs in high schools and summer programs in an effort to recruit more Black kids to their institutions. The goal was to enlarge the African American student body. But these efforts were met with criticism from some parts of the university community, and the most consistent critique was that these students were unqualified. Today this is still one of the most enduring stereotypes in the academy. Special outreach initiatives that focus on bringing more students of color to a university are still met with skepticism. The critics of these initiatives often say that these efforts are unnecessary and that they are an example of "reverse racism" because these programs are giving this group of students unfair access to the university. These efforts were hard for some to accept because they didn't believe in alternate ways of identifying and recruiting talent.

This enduring stereotype of the unqualified African American college student reveals itself in strange ways. When I became a professor at LSU in 1998, I was hired to teach African American history. I love all students and they are drawn to my classes. But on a campus like LSU with about thirty-four thousand students, there were only about ten Black faculty members (it was actually closer to thirty or forty, but I only saw about ten). I remember one day we all went to lunch together, and I said, "Boy, I hope we don't get in a car accident, because if we do, there won't be any Black faculty on campus." In a setting like that, Black students are going to be drawn to African American faculty members, specifically those who are engaging with the students and reaching out. During this period, one of my Black colleagues said to me, "Dr. Moore, I wouldn't have all those Black students in my office at one time." I said, "Why not?" He said, "I also wouldn't have a lot of Black students in my class." I said, "Why not?" He said, "Because then people get the impression that your class is not intellectually rigorous and they think you're just giving grades to Black students." I found that to be completely absurd. My class and my office became a space for Black students to congregate.

The stereotype of the unqualified Black student can also influence when certain classes are offered. There are academic departments across the country that have core classes in the afternoons so that Black athletes can't take those classes because it conflicts with practice. These athletes can't select those majors because they won't be able to take the required courses. The idea of rigor is also perceived to be negatively correlated with the number of Black students and faculty. There's an idea that if a major has too many Black students, if an academic department has too many Black faculty, then somehow the department won't be looked at in the same vein as other departments. This belief is still very pervasive, because Blackness in academia is also perceived to correlate with lowered standards, unqualified students, and diversity agendas. Despite the critiques, many university outreach efforts were successful at increasing the Black student body.

Once on the campus, however, Black students had a litany of grievances. The most prominent was the lack of Black professors and Black teaching assistants. In some disciplines there were no Black professors, no Black TAs, no opportunities for Black students to get engaged in undergraduate research. Black students also wanted Black cultural centers. They wanted a place that gave Black folks a presence and a home on campus. When Black people made these demands, some of the critics focused on Black students' desire to segregate themselves from the larger student body. They wondered why there was a need for a separate Black cultural center when the students should be focused on education. These grievances and critiques still happen to this day.

On some campuses, administrators wanted a certain percentage of the freshman class to be Black. But do you realize that at some major universities, there are still some academic departments that have never hired an African American faculty member? And whenever I'm in those conversations at a conference or some other gathering, the thing they always say is, We can't find any. I say, You can't find any? They're all around. But anyway, that was a complaint then, in 1968, and it's still a complaint now.

Black students also demanded a Black studies major. This was a source of much controversy among professors and administrators. Typically, administrators responded with three major questions or critiques. The first would be about whether there was enough research for a complete major in Black studies. What they were essentially arguing was that Black people had not made a contribution that was worthy of having their experience studied in the academy. The second critique was about staffing. Universities wondered who would teach the courses since there weren't enough "qualified" professors. It's as if they had no idea that HBCUs contained thousands of faculty members who had dedicated their life's work to the study of the Black experience. The third critique was that Black studies didn't have any academic merit or value. This is interesting because although Black studies has become more accepted, it still fights for credibility and legitimacy.

I vividly remember that when I told family and friends I was a history major, they would laugh at me. What you going to do with a history degree? I said, I don't know, but I really love learning and studying about the experiences of Black people. They told me I was crazy, that I wouldn't earn a living, and they would say, "He thinks he's going to be Malcolm X." To me their lack of appreciation for Black studies was a sign of self-hatred. If Black people are discouraging Black students from Black studies, what are we saying about ourselves?

Does Black studies have value? Absolutely. Everybody studies Black folk except Black people themselves. Corporations, data organizations, and finance companies study how Black folks spend their money and time and what their interests are. According to *Black Enterprise*, Black buying power in 2019 was roughly $1.1 trillion and by 2021 it will be close to $1.5 trillion. If Black America were its own country, it would be the fifteenth-wealthiest nation in the world. People study how to grab a piece of that economic pie. If corporations find value in studying Black folks, then we should as well. This is why even now I think Black studies is a great major.

Black students also demanded increased scholarship money. They wanted an increase in pay for janitors and food service workers, who were disproportionately African American. They demanded that universities open their buildings on weekends to give community residents access. They also wanted African American dorms and dining halls, and they wanted Black campus newspapers. They wanted Black resident assistants. When I was a PhD student at Ohio State, I worked as an assistant dorm director for one quarter. It was a really big deal for the Black students in that particular dorm because they finally had someone working there who looked like them. And they would say, "Mr. Moore, you're the first Black assistant or dorm director we've ever had. We don't have any Black RAs. So we're glad you're here, because now we got somebody we can actually talk to."

While Black students were making these demands, they were often asked, "Why don't you go to an HBCU?" Some of them wanted the prestige that went along with going to a PWI. Some felt that their opportunities after graduation would be better if they went to a white school versus an HBCU. Others attended white colleges and universities because their parents and grandparents hadn't been allowed to attend those schools. When we have these HBCU-versus-PWI arguments in the Black middle class, and we have them all the time, I remind people that Black students can go wherever they want. They have that right.

And number two, Black folks were paying taxes to many state institutions for a long time before we had access as students, faculty, and staff.

There are some perks to going to an HBCU. It is one of the few times that a Black person can just be a person. Reflecting on my years at Jackson State with ten thousand Black students, we never had to talk about race. It wasn't even an issue. At an HBCU the professors are Black, the administrators are Black, and the buildings are named after Black people. The history of these institutions is rooted in the Black struggle for freedom and it is woven into the fabric of the institution. When people ask questions about the academic rigor at HBCUs, I remind them that these institutions birthed the Black middle class. More than 50 percent of African Americans with an advanced degree got their undergraduate degree at an HBCU.

These demands from Black students and pushback from administration, faculty, and staff still continue. Many administrators and faculty councils expressed concerns about lowering standards to increase the number of Black students. These critiques generally refer to standardized testing. Ironically, many large white universities in the South did not even require standardized tests as a part of the admissions process. For instance, prior to the integration of the University of Texas at Austin in 1956, standardized tests were not required as a component of the admissions process. But they made that a part of the admissions requirement the same semester that they integrated. Standardized testing has functioned as a racial gatekeeping mechanism for years.

Standardized test scores are correlated with income. The more money a student's family has, the better the student will do on the test. If you come from wealth, there is a strong possibility that you have more exposure. You can take test-prep classes. You can hire private tutors. You can manipulate the disability accommodation exception and get double time on the test. Why in 2021 are we still requiring the SAT or ACT? Are we really basing people's intelligence off of an instrument that was never designed to determine what someone was called to do? Yes, we do it all the time. We limit young people's experiences or opportunities based on a meaningless test score. Is it fair to compare a low-income student to somebody in a wealthier environment who didn't have to work, who didn't have to commute across town on a public bus, who had test-prep classes, who had AP courses at their school, and who had tons of academic support? No, it is not fair to judge them, to compare them, but we do it all the time.

BLACK POWER AND SPORTS

If you watch major college sports today, it is probably hard to believe that at one point many of the football and basketball programs were all-white. The University of Texas football team, which is now approximately 80 percent Black, did not integrate until 1970. And this was typical throughout the South. Comparatively, Ohio State and Michigan had Black players on their teams dating back to the 1890s. But when Southern schools began to integrate their football teams, it was not necessarily a sign of racial progress. In many places it just signaled a change in the business model. Some scholars argue that the legendary Alabama football coach Bear Bryant did more for civil rights than any activist when he integrated the Alabama football team. According to legend, after losing a game to the University of Southern California, Bear Bryant told the university president and boosters, "If we want to be

competitive in college football we need Black players."
They integrated the team the following year.

While Black athletes at Southern schools were just getting onto the campus in the late 1960s, Black athletes at
other places began to articulate their frustrations. They
were not allowed to create their own class schedules.
They were steered toward the noncompetitive majors so
they could focus on their sport. This fed the belief that the
coach held low academic expectations for them. They felt
isolated on campus in a sea of whiteness. They felt and were
treated like gladiators. There were restrictions on their
hairstyles and their clothing, such that at some schools
they were not allowed to wear Afros. They complained that
the coach monopolized all of their time but that once their
playing days were over, the coach and alumni weren't con-
cerned about them. They also complained about how they
were often one of the only Black students in class. Imagine
if you are a six-foot-five, 245-pound Black man and you
walk into a government class. Not only does no one look
like you, but you stand out because of your size and race.

These complaints were not relegated to the 1960s.
During the racial tensions following the murder of George
Floyd, athletes at the University of Texas at Austin published a list of demands calling for building name changes,
statues of Black former UT students, increased funding for
outreach efforts in urban communities, and a statement
against "The Eyes of Texas," the school song that has origins in Jim Crow minstrelsy. Following their lead, Black
athletes at other schools made similar demands about
racial justice, while others added demands about health
and safety issues related to COVID-19.

Just as in the 1960s, many fans were shocked and out-
raged at the athletes' demands. How dare these Black

student athletes complain about racism when they have it so good? It's a privilege to play football at State U. How dare LeBron James speak out against racism? He just needs to shut up and dribble. I want my sports to be free of politics, they say. Well, that ended when they started playing the national anthem at most athletic contests. It went to another level when pro and college teams started partnering with the military to have their teams wear camouflage uniforms and start the game with military flyovers. Politics has always been in sports. People just don't want Black athletes to interject Black politics into it. Part of the reason for this is because white America has always assumed that the Black athlete occupies a position of privilege. When a young football player from the University of Washington says, "We are not your entertainment. We are humans. We are people," it shatters the myth of the privileged Black athlete.

Throughout my years at LSU and UT, many Black student athletes often privately complained about a number of issues. These issues were brought to the surface during the student athlete protests of 2020. As a way to address this frustration, I launched the Black Student-Athlete Summit in 2016, a three-day event for student athletes, administrators, professors, and coaches. In 2019 we had over 500 attendees, and in 2021 we had more than 1,300 attendees who attended virtually. I have yet to meet a Black student athlete who believes that they are privileged because they play a sport in college.

This myth of privilege was largely popularized by the United States Olympic Committee (USOC), which has always used Black athletes as cultural ambassadors. Despite being denied basic human and civil rights, Black athletes have had a constant presence at the Olympics since 1900.

Their presence helped minimize any global perception that the United States was racist. For example, people in 1936 reading about Jesse Owens and the other eight or nine African American athletes competing in the Berlin Olympics would get an impression that the United States was racially progressive because it had Black athletes. This was all part of a strategy to make the country look good on the world stage. And although we celebrate Jesse Owens for winning four gold medals and in the process defeating Hitler's theory of Aryan supremacy, we don't review what happened afterward. After the parades, ceremonies, and press conferences upon his return to the United States, Jesse Owens was back in Cleveland working at a gas station on the Black East Side. After failing to find meaningful employment, he had to humiliate himself by racing against horses just to make a living. The experience of Jesse Owens is very interesting because it showed that the United States would use Black Olympians on the world stage yet then subject them to second-class citizenship at home.

Muhammad Ali became the patron saint for Black athlete activism when he refused induction into the military in 1967. Because of his conversion to the Nation of Islam, he refused based upon his religious and political principles. He famously quipped, "Ain't no Vietcong ever called me a nigger." In an attempt to compromise, the military said that he would just be asked to put on boxing exhibitions for US troops around the globe. Ali refused, was convicted of draft evasion, and was sentenced to prison, although he never served jail time. He was banned from boxing for three years. The sacrifice made by Ali served to inspire generations of African American athletes to use their platform for social change.

As the 1968 Summer Olympics in Mexico City approached, there was a debate in the Black athletic community about whether they should boycott. UCLA's Kareem Abdul-Jabbar, one of the most popular athletes in the country and one of the more vocal Black athletes of his time, decided not to participate. Throughout the discussions, Abdul-Jabbar would talk about his experiences at UCLA and how he was treated differently because he played basketball. If he didn't play basketball, he argued, he would be just another seven-foot Black man dealing with the daily issues of race, like most Black folk did in LA. While Abdul-Jabbar boycotted, other Olympians debated about what course of action to take. They discussed a range of options, from an all-out boycott to participating but doing a protest at the Olympics. Ultimately, they didn't boycott. They understood that the USOC would find suitable replacements for them if they did. Instead they decided to protest on the medal stand when they won events. Tommie Smith and John Carlos did this during their medal ceremony. You have probably seen the iconic photograph of them on the podium with their shoes off, wearing black socks and gloves. As the national anthem played, they gave the Black Power salute on the medal stand. Although they were celebrated in activist and progressive circles back in America, their actions were heavily criticized and they were not recognized as heroes until decades later.

FROM PROTEST TO POLITICS

In the aftermath of MLK's assassination, civil rights activists made a concerted effort to transition from protest to politics. They had been marching for more than a decade and now was the time to seek change through political power. Plus, they wanted to take advantage of several new political developments that would increase their chances for success at the ballot box. First, by 1968 the Voting Rights Act had added several hundred thousand Black voters to the rolls. Second, as white flight continued out of major urban areas, such as Cleveland, Detroit, Newark, and St. Louis, these areas became increasingly Black. Activists could leverage the Black vote at all levels of government. As whites were moving to the suburbs, however, they still wanted to maintain a degree of control over the city. So they came up with two initiatives that were camouflaged as "good government" measures, when in essence they were instruments to dilute Black political power.

The first was an at-large system of voting for city council elections. Most major cities have a ward-based system where the city is divided into wards and each ward elects its own councilperson. But with at-large voting, each councilperson represents the entire city instead of a particular area. For example, if there is a six-person city council, then at election time the six people who get the most votes are on the council. On paper this does not appear problematic; however, at-large voting schemes typically favor middle- to upper-income voters, who have higher rates of political participation than lower-income people. Until recently, Austin, Texas, had an at-large city council voting scheme, in place since the 1950s, and typically more than half of the city council members came from the four wealthiest zip codes in the city.

Second, some cities created a metropolitan form of government that placed all of the power in the hands of a regional body while usurping the power of the city. For example, the city of Miami is controlled by the Miami–Dade County government, which basically replaced the city government with more of a regional or county government.

This effectively stripped officeholders in Miami proper of any power, because suburbanites could vote for their own representatives in their particular locale but then they could also vote for countywide administrators. This system allowed people who moved to the suburbs to control the key assets of many cities.

The transition from protest to politics would pay huge dividends in 1967, when Carl Stokes was elected mayor of Cleveland, making him the first Black mayor of a major American city. This was historic because Cleveland was the poster child of urban decline, deindustrialization, racial tensions, and white flight. Many activists considered the position of mayor to be the most critical in terms of elective appointments. They believed that being mayor of a city was the one position that could immediately address Black grievances. Stokes was not a mayor who happened to be Black; rather, he was a Black mayor. A mayor who happens to be Black is one who governs in a race-neutral fashion, promoting and pushing race-neutral policies, using such excuses as, "Well, my policies help everybody. I can't just look out for Black people." Conversely, a Black mayor is someone whose entire motivation for holding office is to address Black grievances. From 1967 to 1973, Black mayors would be elected in Atlanta, Detroit, Gary, Los Angeles, and several other small to midsize cities. The mayors of these cities came into office determined to use city hall to improve the quality of life for Black people.

When Black mayors take office, they have a clear agenda. First, they want to reform the police department by placing more African Americans in leadership positions and by instituting reforms such as community policing. That's generally number one because of the persistent complaints about police brutality. Second, although they often have no jurisdiction over the public schools, they want to use their power and influence to improve public education. Third, they want to improve the quality of housing for inner-city residents by dispersing public housing to other areas of the city. Fourth, they want to open up employment opportunities for African Americans by requiring firms with city contracts to employ a certain percentage of African American workers. Last, they want to use their office to help African American entrepreneurs.

Mayor Maynard Jackson and the Atlanta airport is a great example of how Black mayors used the powers of their office to create opportunities for Black business owners. When the airport project was launched in 1977, it was the largest construction project in the South. Maynard Jackson made sure 25 percent of the construction contracts went to Black-owned firms. This created a firestorm of controversy. But Jackson insisted, stating that grass would grow on the runways if the city's power structure did not support this initiative. Jackson and the white power structure knew that Atlanta was going to be a hub. They also knew that Atlanta would be home to one of the busiest airports in the country, so Jackson realized that he had an opportunity to get Black business owners a piece of the pie.

He would connect with Black business owners and help them secure contracts. If you think about all of the potential subcontractors needed to build a new airport, the list is endless: flooring, windows, plumbing, cement, lighting, framing, electrical, doors, and more. Additionally, Maynard made sure that Black business owners would be used as suppliers and vendors—paper, soap, lightbulbs, security equipment, concessions—once the airport was built. Maynard Jackson understood that if these minority small business owners could get a contract on the Atlanta airport, then it would open up opportunities for them to bid on larger projects throughout the city, region, and state. Maynard Jackson's efforts created scores of Black millionaires.

Black mayors typically found support among a city's political and economic elites because they were looked upon as insurance policies against race riots. After many of the racial uprisings in the 1960s, some white elites decided to support efforts to elect Black mayors because they knew that racial unrest would create a bad climate for business. They believed that a Black mayor would restore optimism in the Black community, and thus communities would be less likely to take their frustration to the streets.

Although Black mayors had ambitious goals, they didn't anticipate that they would inherit cities with rapidly declining tax bases. As white people moved to the suburbs, they were replaced by poor Black migrants from the South who needed more city services. For example, if the city of Cleveland had six health clinics in 1940, by 1970 they may have needed twelve because a greater percentage of the city was poor. These fiscal realities made it difficult for Black mayors to meet the needs of their citizens, and in many places there were massive cuts in city services. No matter how good or ambitious these mayors were, they had no money to operate. They couldn't function. There were too many people who needed public housing, public transportation, public preschool programs, public recreation, and public health care, and the cities were simply too poor to provide it. The anti-tax movement among the white working class contributed to the decline in the tax base. They had no problem paying taxes as long as those tax dollars went to support public spaces exclusively for their benefit. But they started to complain about paying taxes when they saw their tax money funding services they no longer used or going to welfare programs for the Black poor. This is a critical point. Taxes only became a problem when governmental policies, programs, and initiatives were not exclusively used for white people.

Despite the challenges faced by Black mayors, their elections inspired African Americans to pay attention to electoral politics. On the eve of the 1972 presidential election, over eight thousand Black activists gathered at the National Black Political Convention (NBPC). Held at West Side High School in Gary, Indiana, the NBPC was an effort to end a years-long feud that divided Black America into two distinct camps: integrationists and separatists. While some form of the rift existed long before King's assassination in 1968, his death, and the power vacuum it created, heightened tensions between the two groups. Convention leaders sought to merge these competing ideologies into a national, unified call to action.

During the brief but highly charged three-day meeting, attendees confronted central questions surrounding Black people's involvement in the established political system: Do we reject or accept integration and assimilation? How do we determine the importance or futility of working within the broader white system? And how do we assess the perceived benefits of running for public office? These issues illuminated key differences between integrationists and separatists, yet both sides understood the need to mobilize under a unified platform of Black self-determination.

At the end of the convention, they produced "The National Black Political Agenda," which addressed the Black constituency's priorities. While attendees and delegates agreed with nearly every provision, integrationists maintained their rejection of certain planks, namely support for Palestine, an end to school busing, and separatists' demands for reparations. As a result, Black activists and legislators withdrew their support less than ten weeks after the convention, dashing the hopes of Black nationalists and the NBPC. Despite the collapse of the NBPC, it galvanized entire communities around the possibilities of Black political power, and people went home and ran for public office. One could argue that the presidential victory of Barack Obama and the vice presidential victory of Kamala Harris can be traced back to the energy of the National Black Political Convention.

TEACHING
WHITE LIBERALS

NOW THAT YOU HAVE LEARNED ABOUT THE BLACK experience, let's talk about what to do with the knowledge. Predictably, after the George Floyd and Breonna Taylor murders, many Black people received calls from white colleagues, neighbors, and friends wanting to understand Black frustration. Others were asked by supervisors at work to lead special "diversity initiatives" or workplace discussions to talk about racial injustice in America. Many Black people were essentially being asked to be the Negro Tour Guide at their places of employment, which isn't fair. They are tired. Too many chief diversity officers in corporate America have no budget, no employees, no power, and no influence at their place of employment. They are just figureheads who get a nice title, a pay bump, and a ton of headaches. It's not much better on college campuses. For instance, a few years ago I was approached by a school in the University of California system about their chief diversity officer position. It had the title of vice chancellor, so it sounded fancy and impactful.

While meeting with the committee I asked them what was in the portfolio. They told me it consisted of the Black Cultural Center, the Latino Cultural Center, and the Indigenous Cultural Center. That was it. How could I take a job like that and sit in meetings with other vice chancellors with a tiny and non-impactful portfolio?

In my former capacity as the vice president for diversity and community engagement at the University of Texas at Austin, I was paid to address racial tensions for the entire university community. If it is not in your colleague's job description, however, don't bombard them with a ton of questions. If you do approach your Black colleague and they say, "Not today," don't get offended. It gets exhausting at times. My neighbor came over and brought us some cookies. I appreciated that gesture.

While I, as a Black man, appreciate many of the gestures of support shown for Black Lives Matter by corporations, universities, professional sports leagues, and others in the summer of 2020, we must move beyond performative justice. T-shirts, statements, and slogans written in NFL end zones are good initial steps, but it is not nearly enough if we want to shrink the racial divide. If you are a non-Black person in a position of leadership, then we need you to be courageous when it comes to addressing racial issues either at work or in your community. In my conversations with white executives I have found that when confronted with a racial issue, they do one of three things: one, they act like the issue does not exist; two, if they are forced to acknowledge the issue, then they often put their head in the sand and hope it goes away; and, three, they look for someone to blame (and it is often a Black person). This type of poor leadership is what leads to public relations nightmares for organizations. Part of the problem is rooted in the fact that most white executives don't hire strong Black people for leadership roles. When it comes to positions like chief diversity officers, they often hire someone who is safe, who won't challenge them or the organization, and who is simply happy to have a fancy title and a generous salary. What the executive fails to realize, however, is that they need someone strong, courageous, and bold in the role of chief diversity officer. Why? Because that type of personality in the role will address a racial issue before it reaches the C-suite and before it becomes a media circus. An inability to navigate and manage racial issues in today's climate is a quick way to get fired.

So, if you are in a significant position of leadership, here is my action plan for you. First, you must put considerable resources behind initiatives that improve the racial climate. If these initiatives are not supported by healthy line items in annual or quarterly budgets, then it is a clear sign that you are not committed. Second, hire real Black people. Hire Black people who will challenge you, who will challenge the leadership, and, quite frankly, who will make some people mad. During my time as vice president for diversity and community engagement, I always challenged my peers, deans, and others in visible leadership positions, and they often didn't like it. So what? Additionally, I made it a point to hire activists. Why? Because they always kept me in the loop in terms of how we needed to meet the needs of the university community. Because we had an activist orientation, I prided myself on making sure that we stayed ahead of the curve on potentially hot-button issues. We would address issues proactively. Third, wake up every morning and ask yourself, "What can I do to improve the racial climate within my organization?"

You, as the leader, need to make it a priority. If diversity or anti-racism workshops or trainings are taking place, then you need to be there, engaged, sitting in the front, with your mobile phone turned off. I've discovered that if the leader is present and engaged, then other people will take the session more seriously. Last, make issues of race a strategic priority. In too many strategic plans, improving the racial climate is often relegated to a footnote. It should be a priority until it becomes woven into the fabric of your organization.

For the rest of you, here are six specific steps white Americans (and other non-Black people) can take that involve very little effort. These steps don't require you to admit you're a racist; these steps don't require you to attend a Black Lives Matter march; and these steps don't require you to treat African Americans like they are children. These six practical steps are things you can do immediately to improve America's racial climate.

STEP 1: SEE COLOR

White people often say, "I don't see color." That is a problem. Every semester I have about five to seven Muslim women in my class who wear a hijab. Should I not see them as Muslim? Should I just look at them like I look at every other student? Of course I see them, because I know that wearing a hijab in Texas attracts a ton of harassment. I also have twenty to thirty students who are undocumented in my class. Should I not see them as undocumented? Should I not recognize and acknowledge that their experience is unique? Of course I should. Acknowledging people's lived experience is necessary. So we need you to see color. And that doesn't mean you treat people unfairly; treat everyone fairly but recognize that some people's historical and present-day experiences make it impossible to treat everyone the same.

I told the police officer at my son's middle school that he needed to make a special effort to connect with Black students because of the fractured relationship between Black people and the police. He didn't seem to understand, so I told him pointedly, "Black people for the most part don't trust the police." He said that was unfortunate because he didn't see color. He completely missed the point, but I understand why: he simply can't fathom why African Americans have a distrust of police. Over time we built up a relationship, and one specific conversation let me know that the light, albeit dim, was beginning to turn on for him.

He came up to me after my son's basketball game. "Dr. Moore, thank you for showing me that the Confederate flag was offensive," he said. "Yeah, when you were speaking that day in the library, you talked about it."

"Thanks for letting me know. Do you own a Confederate flag?"

"Yeah, I used to have a flag in my front yard."

"What did you do with it?"

"Well, I took it down." Now, he didn't say he put it in the garage, he didn't say he threw it away, he said he took it down. So hopefully he didn't put it up in the living room.

STEP 2: RECOGNIZE YOUR BIASES

We all have biases. All of us. No matter how liberal you think you are, you have biases that you probably aren't aware of. These biases impact your work, so you need to be conscious of them. Here are some questions to answer about your thoughts and attitudes relative to the Black community:

- When you hear the words Black or African American, what's the first thing you think about?
- What has the media told you about the African American community?
- When you are interviewing Black people for positions, how do you look at their resumes?
- Do you value some schools over others?
- Do you value some high schools over others?
- Do you value certain experiences over others?
- How do you look at GRE scores?
- How do you perceive your Black coworkers?
- How do you perceive your Black students?
- Do you question if your Black coworkers are qualified?
- Do you ever assume that your Black coworker got their job simply because they are Black?
- Do you question their competence?

Here are two examples from my own life of how unconscious bias operates.

In fifth grade, my son took a standardized math test to get into an advanced math class for middle school. He told my wife and me, "I have to get a 75 or 80 to get into the class for sixth grade. It's the first time they're offering it." My wife and I saw it as a great opportunity. He was one of a few kids who passed the test and one of the only Black kids. What did school officials do to the other kids? I was told that to get the other kids into the class, they lowered the minimum score needed to pass. I believe they came to the conclusion that the test was too hard because a bunch of the white students did not pass. But I don't think they did this consciously. I think it was done in a completely unconscious fashion.

The second example came a few years later. In the

eighth grade, my son was one of the best athletes at his school but also an excellent math student. On the first day of school he showed up to his advanced math class and somebody said, "Leonard, what are you doing in here?" They were shocked that he was in the class because they unconsciously thought that Black boys could be great athletes but not great scholars.

STEP 3: STOP STEREOTYPING

I've been a professor for twenty-three years. I got my PhD at twenty-six. I was tenured before I was thirty. I became a full professor before the age of forty, and I hold an endowed professorship. I've been in the game a long time. I was at a faculty senate meeting several years ago and Shaka Smart, then the Texas men's basketball coach, was there giving a presentation about his coaching and academic philosophy. At the end of the meeting a colleague from the English department pointed to me and referred to me as an assistant basketball coach. In his mind I couldn't be a faculty member, I couldn't be an administrator, and I certainly wasn't a vice president. I could only be an assistant basketball coach. Now I always introduce myself as an assistant basketball coach.

Stereotypes have followed me throughout my academic career. One of the joys of my job is that I get to park anywhere on campus, so I typically park right outside the main administrative building in the center of campus. On two separate occasions I was yelled at by parking attendants who told me, "You can't park there!" But when they saw that I had the right parking tag, they apologized. They assumed a Black person couldn't have the all-access parking tag. On another occasion, I was driving through a restricted part of campus. A campus police officer driving in the opposite direction saw the color of my skin and switched lanes to block me. We could've had a head-on collision. But then when he saw that I had the correct parking tag, he started apologizing profusely.

Even when spending time with my family, I have encountered stereotypes. My family and I went to a Texas-Oklahoma game in 2019. We had seats on the forty-five-yard line, sitting about thirty rows up. There was a white family in front of us and the dad, who appeared to be in his late forties, said, "Is your son on the team?"

I replied, "No, my son is next to me."

He said, "Great."

I said, "Is your son on the team?"

He said, "No. Well, did you play at UT?"

"No. Did you play at UT?"

"No."

My wife then said emphatically, "The only reason you are asking those questions is because we are Black and you are trying to figure out how we got these seats. Please turn around and watch the game." It was a helluva mic drop!

STEP 4: CHECK THE MICROAGGRESSIONS

Microaggressions are similar to stereotypes; they are more subtle but equally painful. Recently, a colleague and I were in a meeting and the person we were waiting for walked in, looked at me, and said, "How you doing, Dr. Gordon?" I've been called Dr. Gordon, Dr. Harrison, and Dr. Smith. What do we all have in common? We are all Black men who are professors at the University of Texas at Austin. We look nothing alike. Do you know what it's like to show up to an event and they give you the name badge of another Black person? Black people do not complain, because it doesn't do any good, but we just need to share some of these stories.

A lot of people who claim to be liberal are some of the biggest offenders when it comes to microaggressions and micro-invalidations. Don't assume that all the Black women on campus are there to run track or that the Black men are there to play football or basketball. I had a student who was five-foot-five and he was still stereotyped as a football player. Now, some of you may think, "Well, that's not a bad stereotype," but to the student it is. Because what is being suggested is that the only reason they are on campus is because of their athletic ability.

When I tell white people that I work at the University of Texas at Austin, many of them instinctively think that I work in athletics. After flying in to San Francisco a couple of years ago, my son and I went to the rental car counter. The Avis guy pulled up my information, saw that I worked at the University of Texas at Austin, and said, "Oh, what are you doing out here? Recruiting athletes?"

I said, "No."

"What do you do at UT?"

I said, "Why don't you guess?"

"Well, I don't know. I thought you were out here recruiting."

On several occasions I have arrived at events where I'm the keynote speaker, and typically I'll introduce myself to the organizer just to let them know that I'm there. I'll typically say, "I'm Leonard Moore from the University of Texas." They introduce themselves, and on more than one occasion they will say, "Good to meet you. What time is Dr. Moore coming?" I will say, "I don't know. Hopefully he will be here soon." These are real experiences. If I deal with these things as a Black man, what do my Black female counterparts often deal with? At times microaggressions can become outright hostile for Black women. A Black female colleague was confronted by a white male colleague who stood in her office doorway shortly after she was hired and said, "I don't understand why they're paying you that much money!"

The constant stereotyping and microaggressions confirm what many Black people were told by their parents and grandparents: "You gotta work twice as hard to go half as far." To get ahead in the workplace, we embrace John Henry-ism. "I'm going to just work harder, and harder, and harder, then I'll get the promotion." I was in full-blown John Henry-ism during my years at LSU. A lot of Black professionals take on extra assignments and duties without receiving adequate compensation. We do that because we feel that we have to prove ourselves. But in doing that we work ourselves to death, and we still don't get promoted to the level of our abilities.

STEP 5: GET UNCOMFORTABLE

I want to talk about the importance of getting uncomfortable. Your political affiliation doesn't matter. (You may say you're a liberal, but I know a lot of liberals who value trees and the environment more than people.) Some of us are narrowly trained in our area of expertise but we need specific training around racial injustice. We don't like to go to training because it makes us feel uncomfortable. The first time I went to an anti-sexism training, I was uncomfortable because I didn't realize how a lot of my unconscious actions contributed to sexism. Similarly, many white people don't understand how some of their unconscious actions contribute to an unhealthy racial climate. Anybody can handle budgets or create a strategic plan, but can you navigate the tricky waters of race and racial justice? Discomfort is the fertilizer for growth. If the lived experiences of Black people make you upset, then you need to sit with the discomfort and ask yourself why.

Whenever I teach my Black Power class I always have white alumni sit in on the class. One semester an older white gentleman in his early seventies came to every class. On the last day of class I had him stand up and the students gave him a standing ovation. He said, "Dr. Moore, this has been the greatest experience of my life." In my Race in the Age of Trump class I often have many white students who enroll in the class, but their parents are reluctant to let them take it. One student told me that at the end of every class she would have to take a picture of her notes, email them to her mom, and at night they would discuss the notes as well as the class readings. Apparently, the mom did this because she didn't want her daughter taking my class and "becoming a liberal." By the end of the semester the mom had transformed from a helicopter parent to a convert. She sent me an email and thanked me for changing her perspective.

A way to ease yourself into the discomfort and to learn more about American history, the civil rights movement, and race relations is to do a civil rights tour throughout the great state of Mississippi. You can start in Jackson, Mississippi, at the new civil rights museum, which I think is one of the best museums in the country, and then you can work your way up north through the Mississippi Delta, ending at Memphis, Tennessee. It will be worth your time and money.

STEP 6: "WHAT CAN I HELP YOU FIGHT FOR?"

Many well-meaning white people are often curious about what they can do to help calm racial tensions. Instead of asking, "What can I do?" I recommend you ask a more pro-found question, "What can I help you fight for?"

About ten years ago, I took a group of students from my church to East Austin, which at the time was predom-inantly African American and low-income. Our intent was to canvas the neighborhood and ask residents what issues were important to them. Prior to the outing I asked the students what they thought the community needed. They talked about after-school programs, high-quality childcare, job training programs, a grocery store, more recreational opportunities, and a litany of social programs. They were wrong. The residents of the community wanted speed bumps. Yes, speed bumps. Why? Because a lot of kids in the neighborhood were getting hit by cars during rush hour as commuters used the side streets in East Austin to avoid traffic jams. This was a profound experience for my students, who learned that you must allow a community to tell you what their needs are instead of just assuming you know.

Around the country right now there's a lot of energy on college campuses directed toward taking down Confeder-ate statues and changing building names. But some of that stuff is so woven into the bricks and mortar of an institu-tion that you may never be able to get rid of it all. While I think the typical Black student would agree that these symbolic gestures are important, I believe that they would see other issues as more of a priority. Many of them would like to see an increase in Black enrollment, more Black faculty and staff, and a significant increase in scholarship money for African American students. But many white liberals have co-opted Black activism on America's college campuses to such an extent that the actual demands of

Black students aren't even heard. So we have white liberals expressing what they think is best for Black students without even consulting them.

A few years ago, I was asked to mediate a dispute between a Black law school professor and his disgruntled students, who were upset about a question on an exam. On the exam the professor asked the students to provide a legal defense of school segregation. I thought it was a brilliant question. Before I arrived at the meeting I predicted that the group of angry students were largely white liberals. I was correct. In the group of students I met with, only one was Black. The spokesperson for the group was a white male student who seemed rather happy that he was able to call out his Black professor. The students were up in arms. During our meeting they said the question was "traumatizing" and "triggering" and that they should not be forced to answer it. But it went further. They wanted the professor disciplined. They also demanded that the professor be banned from teaching first-year students and that a committee of faculty approve all of his exam questions moving forward. After listening to their complaints, I said, "This has y'all really upset, huh?" They said, "Yes." Then I asked the following question that changed the entire trajectory of the conversation: "How come you all aren't equally upset that this law school enrolled only ten Black students this year out of an entire class of three hundred?" The room fell silent. In defense of the law students, I believe they meant well. But they were misguided. They got caught up in symbolism and not substance. This is what happens when you assume you know what Black people really want. If you want to really be an ally, to do something radical, ask Black people a simple question: "What can I help you fight for?"

CONCLUSION

WHEN I CHANGED MY MAJOR FROM EDUCATION to history while a freshman at Jackson State University in the spring of 1990, I had no idea what my future would hold. Through teaching Black history, I would travel all over the world; get paid handsome lecture fees; appear on ESPN, CNN, *60 Minutes*, the BBC, and other media outlets; be the subject of a *New York Times* Sunday feature story; be invited to speak with owners from the NFL, NBA, MLB, and NHL; consult with Fortune 100 companies; work with major law firms on large tort cases; and have the opportunity to impact and motivate more than twenty thousand students at Louisiana State University and the University of Texas at Austin. Looking back at my eighteen-year-old self, I was only certain about one thing. I knew that I had no desire to do anything other than teach Black history. I figured that if I was good at it then I could make a good living doing it. Teaching, studying, and writing about the Black experience never gets old. I tell my kids that I have never worked a day in my life, that I have never watched a clock, and that I believe my work has been impactful.

My dad was my first research assistant, and although my mom often questioned why I was in school so long, I know she was proud that her son got his first teaching job at a school in Louisiana that had not allowed her or people who looked like her to attend. After my father passed unexpectedly in 2001, my mom often spent a ton of time with me and my family in Baton Rouge. After being with us a couple of days she would take my car and make the ninety-five-mile drive from my home back to her childhood home in Clifton, right outside Franklinton. Once there she and my grandmother, Ada Warren Burton, would get in the car and drive all over Washington Parish visiting relatives. Whenever I would talk to my grandmother she would always tell me, "Watch out for those white folks at LSU." I did. My mom's trips home were deeply important to her. Clifton was always home to her, and when my sister and brother-in-law moved to Franklinton in 2018 to pastor a church, my Mom was going to relocate with them and spend her last years in the place she was raised. We were all excited for her. We set her room up at my sister's house, made arrangements for her to be involved with other seniors at the local nursing home (where she was related to almost everybody), and purchased her plane ticket. She was going back to where it all started for her in 1938. Unfortunately God had other plans. She took sick and ended up passing in Cleveland. Although she spent more than sixty years of her life in Cleveland, it was never her home.

Conversely, Cleveland was home for my dad. When his parents and siblings moved to Los Angeles in 1961 he stayed behind because he wanted to support the church that his father started. I know that he missed his family. He would talk about how privileged they were to live near one another and how awesome it would be to see his parents and siblings anytime he wanted. We visited Los Angeles often, and my sisters and I would be surrounded by a ton of first cousins. It was like having a family reunion every day. My dad never considered moving to Los Angeles, although I often encouraged him to. I think that at his core he was a product of Cleveland's East Side and he couldn't imagine leaving. My grandfather died in 1974 and my grandmother died in 1984. They are both buried in Los Angeles, hundreds of miles from their respective birthplaces in Mississippi. My dad's life consisted of working at the IRS, being at church—twice on Sundays and many other times during the week—and spending time with his wife and kids. Although he moved the family to Cleveland Heights in the 1960s, he was still a Glenville kid. He would often reminisce about the Moore family in Glenville and the special community it was at that time for Black folks. He deeply missed all of his siblings who moved to Los Angeles. In Cleveland it was just him and his brother Ralph. They were fifteen months apart but they were like twins. When my dad died we buried him at Lake View Cemetery in Cleveland. It was a cemetery I had passed countless times but I hadn't thought they allowed Black folks to get buried there.

Like many other working-class Black parents, Leonard and Peggy Moore promised me and my older sisters that they would pay for us to get a college education, but after that we would be on our own. My oldest sister, Beverly, went to Miami University, and my other sister, Sandra, went to Bowling Green State University. When I decided to go to Jackson State University in the fall of 1989, my parents drove me there. We traveled through Columbus, Cincinnati, Louisville, Nashville, Memphis, and then through the Mississippi Delta before arriving in Jackson for freshman orientation. When they left Jackson two days later they pulled up to the dorm to say goodbye. While I hugged my mom, my dad just put his hand out and said, "Handle yo business." Little did I know that my business would be teaching Black history to white people.

ACKNOWLEDGMENTS

THIS PROJECT WAS THE BRAINCHILD OF AN AMAZing group of people who believe in the power of Black history to change behavior, attitudes, and actions. First, I want to give a special thanks to Kerry Webb from the University of Texas Press, who gave me the idea to turn this into a book. She expressed tremendous faith in the project and her support has been priceless. Second, I want to thank my former Division of Diversity and Community Engagement team, who came up with the idea for these lectures during the racially tense summer of 2020. They are Helen Wormington, Heidi Johnson, Milagros Lopez, Yeo Ju Choi, Jason Molin, and Robert Harrington. Y'all are a great team! I also want to thank the Moores and the Burtons for always sharing their stories. I want to thank my sisters, Sandra and Beverly, who often take my random phone calls as I search for some obscure family history fact. Last, I want to thank the best team around, my wife, Thaïs, and our three kids, Jaaucklyn, Lauryn, and Len.

APPENDIX
SYLLABUS FOR HISTORY OF THE BLACK EXPERIENCE

HISTORY OF THE BLACK EXPERIENCE

This brief course looks at the Black experience in America with a particular emphasis on the period from 1865 to the present. I've chosen to highlight the historical issues and themes that best connect to contemporary Black life in America, putting events like the murder of George Floyd and the growth of Black Lives Matter, as well as debates on topics ranging from policing to reparations, into a much-needed historical context.

BOOKS
Lynch Law in Georgia by Ida B. Wells-Barnett
Negroes with Guns by Robert F. Williams
The Revolt of the Black Athlete: 50th Anniversary Edition
    by Harry Edwards

COURSE OUTLINE
WEEK 1: FREEDOM? (1865-1877)
- The Legacy of Slavery and White Supremacy
- Making Freedom
- Constitutional Amendments
- The Criminalization of Black Life

Read: *The 1619 Project* by Nikole Hannah-Jones, https://
www.nytimes.com/interactive/2019/08/14/magazine/black
-history-american-democracy.html

Watch: https://www.pbs.org/tpt/slavery-by-another-name
/themes/black-codes/

"Laws to Criminalize Black Life?"

"The Origins of Black Codes"

"Pig Laws and Imprisonment"

"New Systems of Exploitation"

WEEK 2: THE NADIR (1877-1940s)

- The Necessity of Jim Crow
- Convict Leasing
- Sharecropping
- Disenfranchisement
- Lynching
- Black Institution Building
- The Lost Cause and Confederate Remembrance

Read: *Lynch Law in Georgia* by Ida B. Wells-Barnett

Watch: https://www.pbs.org/tpt/slavery-by-another-name
/themes/convict-leasing/

"What It Meant to Be a Convict"

"Reflections on Child Convict Labor"

"Reflections on Convict Leasing"

https://www.pbs.org/tpt/slavery-by-another-name/themes
/sharecropping/

"Sharecropping as Slavery"

"The Complications of Sharecropping"

WEEK 3: THE GREAT MIGRATIONS AND THE TRANSFORMATION OF URBAN AMERICA (1920-1965)

- Push/Pull Migration Factors
- White Flight and the Making of Modern Conservatism
- The Making of a Black Underclass

- Redlining and Housing Discrimination
- Employment Bias
- De Facto School Segregation in the Urban North
- Police Brutality

Read: "The Case for Reparations" by Ta-Nehisi Coates, https://www.theatlantic.com/magazine/archive/2014/06/the-case-for-reparations/361631/

Watch: "Redlined: A Legacy of Housing Discrimination," https://www.youtube.com/watch?v=I_sCS2E8k5g

WEEK 4: THE CIVIL RIGHTS MOVEMENT (1954-1965)

- Economic Roots of Black Protest
- Cold War, Civil Rights
- Violent White Resistance
- The Debate over Violence vs. Nonviolence
- Local Movements
- Civil Rights Legislation

Read: *Negroes with Guns* by Robert F. Williams

Watch: "The Murder of Emmett Till," *American Experience*, https://www.pbs.org/video/the-murder-of-emmett-till-j6dpye/

"Fannie Lou Hamer Interview 1965," https://www.youtube.com/watch?v=-a3KqhkPQ-s

WEEK 5: THE BLACK POWER MOVEMENT (1965-1972)

- Northern Urban Frustration
- The Impact of the Nation of Islam
- The Revolutionary Nature of the Black Panther Party
- Black Power and the College Campus
- COINTELPRO
- The Rise of Black Political Power

Read: *The Revolt of the Black Athlete: 50th Anniversary Edition* by Harry Edwards

"The Rank and File Women of the Black Panther Party and Their Powerful Influence" by Janelle Harris Dixon, https://www.smithsonianmag.com/smithsonian-institution/rank-and-file-women-black-panther-party-their-powerful-influence-180971591/

Watch: "Malcolm X's Legendary Speech: 'The Ballot or the Bullet,'" https://www.youtube.com/watch?v=8zLQLUpNGsc

WEEK 6: BLACK LIFE AND THE CONSERVATIVE COUNTERREVOLUTION (1980s–PRESENT)

- The Privatization, Segregation, and End of Public Education
- Gentrification
- Mass Incarceration and the New Jim Crow
- Voter Suppression in the Age of Trump

Watch: *13th*, https://www.youtube.com/watch?v=krfcq5pF8u8

Read: "Austin's Gentrification Problem: How We Got Here" by Ashley Goudeau, https://www.kvue.com/article/news/local/austins-gentrification-problem-how-we-got-here/269-548075155

"The New Jim Crow: How the War on Drugs Gave Birth to a Permanent American Undercaste" by Michelle Alexander, https://www.thenation.com/article/archive/new-jim-crow/

"'They Don't Really Want Us to Vote': How Republicans Made It Harder" by Danny Hakim and Michael Wines, https://www.nytimes.com/2018/11/03/us/politics/voting-suppression-elections.html

SUGGESTED READING

AFRICAN AMERICAN HISTORY OVERVIEWS

Berry, Daina Ramey, and Kali Nicole Gross. *A Black Women's History of the United States*. Boston: Beacon Press, 2020.

Franklin, John Hope, and Evelyn Brooks Higginbotham. *From Slavery to Freedom: A History of African Americans*. 9th ed. New York: McGraw-Hill, 2010.

Harding, Vincent. *There Is a River: The Black Struggle for Freedom in America*. Boston: Harcourt Brace, 1981.

Kendi, Ibram X. *Stamped from the Beginning: The Definitive History of Racist Ideas in America*. New York: Bold Type Books, 2017.

Kendi, Ibram X., and Keisha N. Blain. *Four Hundred Souls: A Community History of African America, 1619–2019*. New York: One World, 2021.

SLAVERY AND EMANCIPATION

Baptist, Edward E. *The Half Has Never Been Told: Slavery and the Making of American Capitalism*. New York: Basic Books, 2014.

Berlin, Ira. *Many Thousands Gone: The First Two Centuries of Slavery in North America*. Cambridge, MA: Belknap Press, 1998.

Berry, Daina Ramey. *The Price for Their Pound of Flesh: The Value of the Enslaved, from Womb to Grave, in the Building of a Nation.* Boston: Beacon Press, 2017.

Du Bois, W. E. B. *Black Reconstruction in America, 1860–1880.* Oxford, UK: Oxford University Press, 2007.

Finkelman, Paul. *Slavery and the Founders: Race and Liberty in the Age of Jefferson.* Abingdon, UK: Routledge, 2014.

Foner, Eric. *The Second Founding: How the Civil War and Reconstruction Remade the Constitution.* New York: W. W. Norton, 2020.

Genovese, Eugene D. *Roll, Jordan, Roll: The World the Slaves Made.* New York: Random House, 1974.

Gomez, Michael A. *Exchanging Our Country Marks: The Transformation of African Identities in the Colonial and Antebellum South.* Chapel Hill: University of North Carolina Press, 1998.

Hurston, Zora Neale. *Barracoon: The Story of the Last "Black Cargo."* New York: Amistad Press, 2018.

Jacobs, Harriet. *Incidents in the Life of a Slave Girl.* Reprint ed. Mineola, NY: Dover, 2001.

Johnson, Walter. *Soul by Soul: Life Inside the Antebellum Slave Market.* Cambridge, MA: Harvard University Press, 2000.

Litwack, Leon F. *Been in the Storm So Long: The Aftermath of Slavery.* New York: Alfred A. Knopf, 1979.

McLaurin, Melton A. *Celia, a Slave.* Athens: University of Georgia Press, 1991.

Mellon, James. *Bullwhip Days: The Slaves Remember; An Oral History.* New York: Grove Press, 1988.

Morgan, Edmund S. *American Slavery, American Freedom: The Ordeal of Colonial Virginia.* Paperback reissue. New York: W. W. Norton, 2003.

Northup, Solomon. *Twelve Years a Slave.* Mineola, NY: Dover, 2000.

Oubre, Claude F. *Forty Acres and a Mule: The Freedmen's Bureau and Black Land Ownership.* Baton Rouge: Louisiana State University Press, 2012.

Smallwood, Stephanie E. *Saltwater Slavery: A Middle Passage from Africa to American Diaspora*. Cambridge, MA: Harvard University Press, 2007.

Stuckey, Sterling. *Slave Culture: Nationalist Theory and the Foundations of Black America*. Oxford, UK: Oxford University Press, 2013.

Thomas, Hugh. *The Slave Trade: The Story of the Atlantic Slave Trade, 1440–1870*. New York: Simon and Schuster, 1999.

White, Deborah Gray. *Ar'n't I a Woman? Female Slaves in the Plantation South*. Rev. ed. New York: W. W. Norton, 1999.

Wilentz, Sean. *No Property in Man: Slavery and Antislavery at the Nation's Founding*. With new preface. Cambridge, MA: Harvard University Press, 2018.

Williams, Eric. *Capitalism and Slavery*. 3rd ed. Chapel Hill: University of North Carolina Press, 2021.

JIM CROW AND SEGREGATION

Allen, James. *Without Sanctuary: Lynching Photography in America*. 14th ed. Twin Palms, 2020.

Bay, Mia. *Traveling Black: A Story of Race and Resistance*. Cambridge, MA: Belknap Press, 2021.

Bond, Horace Mann, and Julia W. Bond. *The Star Creek Papers: Washington Parish and the Lynching of Jerome Wilson*. Athens: University of Georgia Press, 1997.

Gates, Henry Louis, Jr. *Stony the Road: Reconstruction, White Supremacy, and the Rise of Jim Crow*. London: Penguin Press, 2019.

Higginbotham, Evelyn Brooks. *Righteous Discontent: The Women's Movement in the Black Baptist Church, 1880–1920*. Rev. paperback ed. Cambridge, MA: Harvard University Press, 1994.

LeFlouria, Talitha L. *Chained in Silence: Black Women and Convict Labor in the New South*. Chapel Hill: University of North Carolina Press, 2015.

Litwack, Leon F. *Trouble in Mind: Black Southerners in the Age of Jim Crow*. New York: Alfred A. Knopf, 1998.

Norrell, Robert J. *Up from History: The Life of Booker T. Washington*. Cambridge, MA: Belknap Press, 2009.

Oshinsky, David M. *"Worse Than Slavery": Parchman Farm and the Ordeal of Jim Crow Justice*. New York: Free Press, 1997.

Parker, Alison M. *Unceasing Militant: The Life of Mary Church Terrell*. Chapel Hill: University of North Carolina Press, 2020.

Reed, Touré F. *Not Alms but Opportunity: The Urban League and the Politics of Racial Uplift, 1910-1950*. Chapel Hill: University of North Carolina Press, 2008.

Seidule, Ty. *Robert E. Lee and Me: A Southerner's Reckoning with the Myth of the Lost Cause*. New York: St. Martin's Press, 2021.

Sullivan, Patricia. *Lift Every Voice: The NAACP and the Making of the Civil Rights Movement*. New York: New Press, 2010.

Touri, Rebecca. *Strategic Sisterhood: The National Council of Negro Women in the Black Freedom Struggle*. Chapel Hill: University of North Carolina Press, 2018.

Walker, Vanessa Siddle. *Their Highest Potential: An African American School Community in the Segregated South*. Chapel Hill: University of North Carolina Press, 1996.

BLACK URBANIZATION

Baldwin, Davarian L. *Chicago's New Negroes: Modernity, the Great Migration, and Black Urban Life*. Chapel Hill: University of North Carolina Press, 2007.

Hirsch, Arnold R. *Making the Second Ghetto: Race and Housing in Chicago, 1940-1960*. Cambridge, UK: Cambridge University Press, 1983.

Kruse, Kevin M. *White Flight: Atlanta and the Making of Modern Conservatism*. Princeton, NJ: Princeton University Press, 2007.

Lemann, Nicholas. *The Promised Land: The Great Black Migration and How It Changed America*. New York: Alfred A. Knopf, 1991.

Moore, Leonard N. *Black Rage in New Orleans: Police Brutality and African American Activism from World War II to Hurricane Katrina*. Baton Rouge: Louisiana State University Press, 2010.

Rothstein, Richard. *The Color of Law: A Forgotten History of How Our Government Segregated America*. New York: Liveright, 2017.

Taylor, Keeanga-Yamahtta. *Race for Profit: How Banks and the Real Estate Industry Undermined Black Homeownership*. Chapel Hill: University of North Carolina Press, 2019.

Wilkerson, Isabel. *The Warmth of Other Suns: The Epic Story of America's Great Migration*. New York: Random House, 2010.

CIVIL RIGHTS

Bell, Janet Dewart. *Lighting the Fires of Freedom: African American Women in the Civil Rights Movement*. New York: New Press, 2018.

Blain, Keisha N. *Until I Am Free: Fannie Lou Hamer's Enduring Message to America*. Boston: Beacon Press, 2021.

Charron, Katherine Mellen. *Freedom's Teacher: The Life of Septima Clark*. Chapel Hill: University of North Carolina Press, 2009.

Cosgrove, Stuart. *Memphis 68: The Tragedy of Southern Soul*. Edinburgh, UK: Polygon, 2017.

Garrow, David J. *Bearing the Cross: Martin Luther King, Jr., and the Southern Christian Leadership Conference*. New York: William Morrow, 2004.

Lavergne, Gary M. *Before* Brown: *Heman Marion Sweatt, Thurgood Marshall, and the Long Road to Justice*. Austin: University of Texas Press, 2011.

Monteith, Sharon. *SNCC's Stories: The African American*

Freedom Movement in the Civil Rights South. Athens: University of Georgia Press, 2020.

Moody, Anne. *Coming of Age in Mississippi: The Classic Autobiography of Growing Up Poor and Black in the Rural South*. New York: Dell, 1992.

Ransby, Barbara. *Ella Baker and the Black Freedom Movement: A Radical Democratic Vision*. Chapel Hill: University of North Carolina Press, 2003.

Robinson, Jo Ann Gibson. *The Montgomery Bus Boycott and the Women Who Started It: The Memoir of Jo Ann Gibson Robinson*. Edited by David J. Garrow. Knoxville: University of Tennessee Press, 1987.

Rolph, Stephanie R. *Resisting Equality: The Citizens' Council, 1954–1989*. Baton Rouge: Louisiana State University Press, 2018.

BLACK POWER

Biondi, Martha. *The Black Revolution on Campus*. Berkeley: University of California Press, 2012.

Bradley, Stefan M. *Upending the Ivory Tower: Civil Rights, Black Power, and the Ivy League*. New York: New York University Press, 2018.

Edwards, Harry. *The Revolt of the Black Athlete: 50th Anniversary Edition*. Champaign: University of Illinois Press, 2018.

Farmer, Ashley D. *Remaking Black Power: How Black Women Transformed an Era*. Chapel Hill: University of North Carolina Press, 2019.

Favors, Jelani M. *Shelter in a Time of Storm: How Black Colleges Fostered Generations of Leadership and Activism*. Chapel Hill: University of North Carolina Press, 2020.

Joseph, Peniel E. *The Sword and the Shield: The Revolutionary Lives of Malcolm X and Martin Luther King Jr*. New York: Basic Books, 2020.

——. *Waiting 'Til the Midnight Hour: A Narrative History of Black Power in America*. New York: Henry Holt, 2006.

Moore, Leonard N. *The Defeat of Black Power: Civil Rights and the National Black Political Convention of 1972*. Baton Rouge: Louisiana State University Press, 2018.

Payne, Les, and Tamara Payne. *The Dead Are Arising: The Life of Malcolm X*. New York: Liveright, 2020.

Rhoden, William C. *Forty Million Dollar Slaves: The Rise, Fall, and Redemption of the Black Athlete*. New York: Crown, 2006.

Rojas, Fabio. *From Black Power to Black Studies: How a Radical Social Movement Became an Academic Discipline*. Baltimore, MD: Johns Hopkins University Press, 2007.

Seale, Bobby. *Seize the Time: The Story of the Black Panther Party and Huey P. Newton*. Reprint ed. Baltimore, MD: Black Classic Press, 1996.

Shakur, Assata. *Assata: An Autobiography*. Chicago: Lawrence Hill Books, 2001.

Smethurst, James Edward. *The Black Arts Movement: Literary Nationalism in the 1960s and 1970s*. Chapel Hill: University of North Carolina Press, 2005.

Spencer, Robyn C. *The Revolution Has Come: Black Power, Gender, and the Black Panther Party in Oakland*. Durham, NC: Duke University Press, 2016.

Taylor, Ula Yvette. *The Promise of Patriarchy: Women and the Nation of Islam*. Chapel Hill: University of North Carolina Press, 2017.

X, Malcolm. *The Autobiography of Malcolm X: As Told to Alex Haley*. New York: Ballantine Books, 1992.

RACE, SOCIETY, AND ANTI-RACISM

DiAngelo, Robin. *White Fragility: Why It's So Hard for White People to Talk about Racism*. Boston: Beacon Press, 2020.

Fleming, Crystal M. *How to Be Less Stupid about Race: On Racism, White Supremacy, and the Racial Divide*. Boston: Beacon Press, 2018.

Kendi, Ibram X. *How to Be an Antiracist*. New York: One
    World, 2019.

Oluo, Ijeoma. *So You Want to Talk about Race*. New York: Seal
    Press, 2018.

Wilkerson, Isabel. *Caste: The Origins of Our Discontents*. New
    York: Random House, 2020.

INDEX

Abdul-Jabbar, Kareem, 141
academia, 156
Adams, John, 51
admissions policies, 7-8, 159-160
adoption, 11
advanced degrees, 97-98, 136
affirmative action, 7-8
Affordable Care Act, 48
African American History (course), 19
African American Literature (course), 19
African diaspora, 128
Africans in Louisiana Tours, 46
after-school programs, 159
agriculture, 41. *See also* cotton cultivation
airport project (Atlanta), 144-145
Alabama: and American slave system, 43; and antigovernment sentiment, 101, 102; forced sterilization of Black women, 117. *See also specific cities*
Alabama Christian Movement for Human Rights, 115
Albany, Georgia, 114

Ali, Muhammad, 140
Ali, Noble Drew, 122
Amtrak, 80
Anniston, Alabama, 96, 114-115
antigovernment sentiment, 101-102
antitax sentiment, 101-102
apartment housing, 92
appraisals of houses, 94
Arabic names, 123
Arkansas, 43
Aryan supremacy, 140
assassinations, 52, 126-127, 131, 141, 146. *See also* lynchings
athletes and athletics. *See* sports
Atlanta, Georgia, 70, 143-145
Atlanta Journal, 70
Atlantic slave trade, 43
at-large voting, 142
Austin, Texas, 52-53, 93, 142, 159
automation, 86
aviation industry, 83

Bailey County, Texas, 35-36
Baker, Ella, 109-110, 113
banking practices, 91-92, 94
Bass, Thaïs, 21

Baton Rouge, Louisiana, 45–46, 93, 162

Beaumont, Texas, 101, 102

Berlin Olympic Games, 140

biases, 8, 152–154. *See also* discrimination; stereotypes

Bible studies, 53–54

Bilbo, Theodore, 63

Birmingham, Alabama, 115–116

Black activism, 24, 75

Black businesses, 73–74, 80–81, 144

Black Codes, 55–56

Black cultural centers, 133, 149

Black Enterprise, 134–135

Black faculty, 133–135, 159–160

Black Greeks (fraternities), 94

Black History Month, 19, 23, 27

Black Lives Matter: and author's class curricula, 23, 27–28; criticisms of, 115; establishment support for, 149; goals of, 113; King's tactics compared to, 112

Black mayors, 143–146

Black Monday (Brady), 102–106

Black newspapers, 19, 82, 95, 120, 125–126

Black Panther Party, 128–131

black power: and Black Panther Party, 128–131; and higher education, 131–137; and Malcolm X, 125–127; and the Nation of Islam, 122–125, 125–127; and political activism, 141–147; and sports, 137–141; and the summer of 1965, 120–121

Black Power (course), 1, 26–27, 36, 158

Black Reconstruction, 47

Black Student-Athlete Summit, 139

Black studies, 134–135

Black Wall Street, 74

blockbusting, 92–93

Bloody Sunday, 119

Boeing, 83

Bogalusa, Louisiana, 105

boll weevils, 77–78

Boston, Massachusetts, 78

Bowling Green State University, 163

boycotts, 104, 106–108, 141

Boynton v. Virginia, 114

Brady, Tom, 102–103

Brown, Elaine, 130

Brown, H. Rap, 5, 19

Brown, Michael, 1

Brown, Will, 68

Brown v. Board of Education, 85, 98–99, 100–101

Bryant, Bear, 137

Burton, Ada Warren, 83, 162

business school students, 5, 14–15

"Cancer Alley," 102

capitalism, 43, 128

career fairs, 24

Carlos, John, 141

Carmichael, Stokely, 19

Case Western Reserve University, 20, 96

causes and justifications for slavery, 40–41

Chaney, James, 118

Charleston, South Carolina, 44

Charlotte, North Carolina, 71

chattel slavery, 41

Chauvin, Derek, 32, 33

chauvinism, 107

Chicago, Illinois, 27, 78, 84

childcare programs, 159

Chinese immigrants, 25

Chowchilla, California, 105

Christianity, 39, 40–41, 53–54, 123–124

churches: Church of God in Christ, 73; and community activism, 159; Dexter Avenue Baptist Church, 107; and Jim Crow, 60; and King's background, 127; and legacy of plantation system, 53–54; and myths of civil rights movement, 115; and the Nation

of Islam, 124; Sixteenth Street Baptist Church, 116; St. James Missionary Baptist Church, 81; white supremacist violence against, 116. *See also* religion
city governments, 143-144
City of New Orleans (train), 80
city services, 145. *See also* public housing; public transportation
Civil Rights Act of 1964, 32, 116, 118-119
civil rights movement: and Black Panther Party, 128-131; civil rights legislation, 32, 54, 56, 57-58, 62; civil rights mobilizers vs. organizers, 109-111; combating public transportation segregation, 106-108; and impact of World War II, 95-96; key civil rights organizations, 73, 113-119; and legacy of Civil War, 51-52; Nation of Islam critiques of, 126; and school segregation, 84-85, 97-102, 102-106; and sit-in movement, 111-112; white resistance, 102-106
civil rights museums, 158
Civil War: and American slave system, 43; and Black people's transition to freedom, 48-54; and Field Order No. 15, 52; legacy on race relations, 51-52; and Lost Cause ideology, 74-76; and slave population of the South, 43; and Southern white society, 47-48
Clark, Septima, 110
Clarksville, Texas, 34
class divisions, 15-16, 47-48, 81-83, 83-84, 90-91
Cleveland, Ohio: and author's class curricula, 27; and author's family background, xv, 16, 17-20, 162-163; and Black mayors, 143, 145; and housing discrimination,

89; and migration of Black Southerners, 73, 78-79; and the Nation of Islam, 125; and Owens' post-Olympics life, 140; and public school segregation, 85; racial background, 19; and voter mobilization, 64; and white flight, 142
Cleveland Call and Post, 19
Cleveland Heights, Ohio, 18, 88, 163
Cleveland Public Library, 20
Cleveland State University, 20
Clifton, Louisiana, 71, 81, 162
CNN, 1
Cold War, 110
colonial America, 40
Columbia University, 97
Colvin, Claudette, 107
community organizations, 73-74, 128-129
Compromise of 1877, 58
Confederate flag, 25, 103, 152
Confederate monuments and statues, 74-76, 103, 159-160
Congress of Racial Equality (CORE), 113, 121
Connor, Bull, 115-116
conservatism, 3, 5, 25
controversies surrounding Black history, xiv, 26-27
conversion, religious, 40-41, 124
convict leasing, 67-68, 69
corporations, 14, 135
cotton cultivation, 44-45, 55, 62, 77-78
COVID-19 pandemic, 25, 38, 138
criminal justice, 67-68
Crispus Attucks High School, 78
cultural ambassadors, 139
cultural intelligence, 51

Dallas, Texas, 13
Davis, Angela, 19, 20, 130
Deacons for Defense and Justice, 105
debt/indebtedness, 31-32, 81-82

Declaration of Independence, 42, 59
Deep South, xiv, 43, 44, 87
de facto segregation, 84-85
deindustrialization, 86, 143
de jure segregation, 84
Detroit, Michigan, 27, 78, 142, 143
Die Nigger Die (Brown), 5
dietary laws, 124
discomfort with race issues, 157-158
discrimination, 7, 8, 30-32
disease immunity, 40
disenfranchisement of Blacks, 62-65
diversity in education, 2-5, 131-133,
     148-149
Division of Diversity and Commu-
     nity Engagement, 22
domestic labor, 108
domestic slave trade, 44-45, 49-50
Double V campaign, 95-96
Douglass, Frederick, 43
driving while Black, 34-38
Du Bois, W. E. B., 47

economic impact of Black culture,
     135, 144
economic intimidation, 104
economic structure of the South,
     47-48
education: and author's background,
     19-21; and author's family
     background, 163; and Blacks'
     transition to freedom, 53; diver-
     sity in education, 2-5, 131-133,
     148-149; and Free Breakfast for
     Children, 129; K-12 education,
     97, 99; power of, 25-26. *See also*
     historically black colleges and
     universities (HBCUs); school
     segregation
election laws, 62-65. *See also*
     disenfranchisement of Blacks;
     voting rights
El-Hajj Malik El-Shabazz, 127. *See
     also* X, Malcolm
Emancipation Proclamation, 48-50

employment discrimination, 85-87
"enslaved Africans," 39
Evergreen Plantation, 45
"Eyes of Texas, The," 138

family background of author, xv-
     xvi, 16-20, 78-79, 162-163
family separations, 49-50
Federal Housing Administration
     (FHA), 91
Ferguson, Missouri, 1-2
Field Order No. 15 ("Forty Acres
     and A Mule"), 52
Fifteenth Amendment, 54, 57-58, 62
Floyd, George: and author's class
     curricula, 27-28; protests in-
     spired by death of, 104, 121, 138;
     and racial injustice dialogue,
     148; and systemic racism, 32-33
forced sterilization of Black women,
     117
Fort McClellan, 96
"Forty Acres and A Mule" (Field
     Order No. 15), 52
founding fathers, 42
Fourteenth Amendment, 54, 57-58,
     62
Franklinton, Louisiana: and
     author's background, xv; Black
     cemeteries, 59; lynchings,
     71; and migration of Black
     Southerners, 79, 83; and school
     segregation, 101
fraternities, 3, 9, 94
Frazier, Garrison, 51-52
Free Breakfast for Children, 129
freedmen communities, 52-53
freedom rides, 113, 114
freedom schools, 116-117
Freedom Summer, 116-118
Freemasonry, 122
fugitive slaves, 43, 48-49

Garvey, Marcus, 122
Gary, Indiana, 143

gatekeeping, 136–137
gender norms, 107, 124–125, 129–131, 156–157
geography, 41
Georgia, 43, 51, 52, 69–70. *See also specific cities*
"good government" measures, 142
Goodman, Andrew, 118
graduate studies, 20, 97–98, 136
Grambling State University, 61
grandfather clauses, 62–63
Great Migration: and author's family background, xvi; and class divisions among Blacks, 83–84; and housing discrimination, 89–90; push and pull factors, 77–81; white resistance to, 81–83
Greek culture (fraternities), 3, 94
Green-Meldrim House, 51–52
Greenwood, Mississippi, 56–57
Griffin, Georgia, 70
gun rights, 105–106, 128. *See also* self-defense

hair styles, 12, 138
Hamer, Fannie Lou, 117–118
harassment, 35. *See also* police misconduct and violence
Harris, Kamala, 147
Hayes, Rutherford B., 58
health services, 145
Hebrew schools, 18–19
Henry, Patrick, 42
higher education, 131–137
Highlander Folk School, 110
high school curricula, 27
hijab, 151
hiring practices, 149–150
historically black colleges and universities (HBCUs): advantages of, 136; and author's class curricula, 8; and author's teaching career, 3; and Black institution building during Jim Crow, 73; and Black Power organizations, 131; and

Black students from the North, 80; and push for Black studies majors, 134; and segregation of Texas universities, 97; and sit-in movement, 111
historiography, 20
History of Black Power Movement (course), 3–10, 10–12, 12–14
Hitler, Adolf, 140
Holocaust education, 19, 26
homeownership, 52, 88–94
Hose, Sam, 69–70
housing discrimination, 88–94
Huggins, Ericka, 130
hysterectomies, forced, 117

Illinois, 85. *See also* Chicago, Illinois
immigrants and immigration, 24–25
importance of Black history, xiii–xiv, 26
income inequality, 136–137
indentured servitude, 41
Indianapolis, Indiana, 78–79
indictments, 33
Indigenous Cultural Center, 149
inherent biases, 152–154
inner city areas, 22, 87, 129
institutional racism, 32–33
integration: and civil rights organizations, 114; and college sports, 137–138; and goals of civil rights organizations, 121; and the National Black Political Convention (NBPC), 146; Nation of Islam critiques of, 126; of schools, 84–85, 111
intelligence tests, 8, 137
intergenerational effects of slavery, 44–45, 49–50
Interstate Commerce Commission, 115
Interstate Highways Act, 90
interstate highway system, 90
IQ tests, 8
Israel, 83

Jackson, Andrew, 51

Jackson, Jesse, 112

Jackson, Maynard, 144–145

Jackson, Mississippi, 56–57, 71, 108, 158

Jackson State University: and advantages of HBCUs, 136; and author's background, 19, 161, 163–164; and Black students from the North, 80; and legacy of plantation system, 56; and Montgomery Bus Boycott, 108

Jakes, Thomas Dexter, 8

James, LeBron, 138

Jefferson, Thomas, 42, 51

Jesus, 53–54

Jet, 104

Jews and Judaism, 11, 18–19, 26

Jim Crow: and author's class curricula, 7; and Black institution building, 72–74; and civil rights organizations, 113, 116; and class divisions among Blacks, 83–84; and Confederate monument controversies, 74–76; and convict leasing, 67–68, 69; and disenfranchisement of Blacks, 62–65; and economic control of Blacks, 65–68; informal codes of, 60–61; legacy of, in contemporary society, 67; and legacy of plantation system, 55–58; and lynchings, 61, 68–72; and military service of Blacks, 96, 97; and minstrelsy, 138; and *Plessy v. Ferguson*, 100; scope of, 59; and sit-in movement, 111; state-specific laws, 59–60. *See also* segregation

job discrimination, 85–87

"John Henry-ism," 157

Johnson, Andrew, 52, 55

Johnson, Lyndon Baines, 119

Jones, Ralph Waldo Emerson, 61

Juneteenth celebrations, 49

K-12 education, 97, 99

Kennedy, John F., 115, 126–127

King, Martin Luther, Jr.: assassination, 131, 141, 146; background, 127; and civil rights organizations, 113–115; criticisms of, 112; and mobilizers vs. organizers, 109–110; and Montgomery Bus Boycott, 106–108

Ku Klux Klan (KKK), 13, 58, 116

Kwanzaa, 19

Lake View Cemetery, 163

Lakeway suburb, 22–23

land ownership, 51–52. *See also* homeownership

Latino Cultural Center, 149

law schools, 160

LD (learning disability) classes, 84

leadership roles, 149–150

liberals and liberalism: advice to white allies, 158–160; and author's class, 2; and George Floyd murder, 33; and inherent biases, 152; and responses to author's class, 6; and stereotypes and microaggressions, 156; and value of discomfort, 157–158

light-skin Blacks, 12

Lincoln, Abraham, 52

literacy, 62, 66

Los Angeles, California: and author's family background, 78–79, 162–163; and Black history curricula, 27; and Black mayors, 143; and migration of Black Southerners, 78–79, 80, 82, 84

Los Angeles Police Department, 34

Los Angeles Sentinel, 120

Los Angeles Times, 120

Lost Cause ideology, 74–76

Louisiana: and American slave system, 43; and antigovernment sentiment, 101, 102; and disenfranchisement of Blacks, 65; forced sterilization of Black women, 117; and legacy of plantation system, 45-46, 56-58; and Lost Cause ideology, 75; and migration of Black Southerners, 73-74, 80. *See also specific cities*

Louisiana Purchase, 43-44

Louisiana State University (LSU): Afeni Shakur lecture, 130-131; and author's family background, 162; and author's teaching career, xiv-xvi, 21, 83, 161; Black power and college sports, 139; collaboration with US Army Corps of Engineers, 56; and glorification of plantations, 46; and stereotypes and microaggressions, 157; teaching Black history in the South, 21

lynchings: and author's background, xv; and author's class curricula, 7; as backlash against *Brown* decision, 104-105; of Black veterans, 96; documentation of, 68-72; and informal codes of Jim Crow, 61; and migration of Black Southerners, 82

Madison, James, 42

Managing in the Age of George Floyd and Breonna Taylor (webinar), 29-30, 38

Many, Louisiana, 105

Marshall, Thurgood, 98

Maryland, 43

mathematics, 154

McCallum High School, 23

McComb, Mississippi, 103

McDonnell Douglas, 83

Mecca, Saudi Arabia, 127

media, 13, 161. *See also* Black newspapers

Merritt College, 128

Miami, Florida, 142-143

Miami-Dade County, Florida, 142-143

Miami University, 163

Michigan State Capitol, 106

Michigan State University, 137

microaggressions, 155-157

migration of Blacks, 77-81

military service of Blacks, 77

Milwaukee, Wisconsin, 78

Minneapolis Police Department, 33

minstrelsy, 138

Mississippi: and American slave system, 43; and antigovernment sentiment, 101, 102; and disenfranchisement of Blacks, 65; forced sterilization of Black women, 117; and Freedom Summer, 116-118; and Jim Crow, 60; and legacy of plantation system, 57. *See also specific cities*

"Mississippi appendectomy," 117

Mississippi Delta, 56

Mobile, Alabama, 44

mobilizers vs. organizers, 109-111, 126

Money, Mississippi, 104

Monopoly (game), 30-32

Monroe, James, 42, 51

Monroe, North Carolina, 105

Montgomery, Alabama, 119

Montgomery Bus Boycott, 106-108, 112

Montgomery Improvement Association, 108

Moore, Bessie Lee, 78

Moore, Ezekiel, 78

Moore, Leonard, 163

Moore, Peggy, 163

Moore, Ralph, 163

Moore, Sheila, 20

Moore family background, xv-xvi, 78-79, 162-163

mortgage programs, 91

Muhammad, Elijah, 125-126

Muhammad Speaks, 125-126

multifamily housing units, 92
murder, 118. *See also* assassinations; lynchings
museums, 76
myth of privilege, 139

names of formerly enslaved people, 50–51, 123
nannies, 11–12
National Association for the Advancement of Colored People (NAACP): and activism of Black veterans, 96; and Black self-defense, 105; and civil rights activism outside the South, 121; goals and tactics of, 113; and mobilizers vs. organizers, 109; and school desegregation campaign, 97–99
National Baptist Convention, 73
"The National Black Political Agenda" (NBPC), 146–147
National Black Political Convention (NBPC), 146
Nation of Islam, 122–125, 125–127, 140
Negroes with Guns (Williams), 5
Newark, New Jersey, 79–80, 142
New Jersey, 85. *See also* Newark, New Jersey
Newnan, Georgia, 70
New Orleans, Louisiana, 44, 80
Newton, Huey, 128
New York City, 27, 78, 84
New York State, 85
New York Times, 71, 161
Nigerian Americans, 13
nonviolent resistance, 121, 126
North Carolina, 43, 51, 52, 109. *See also specific cities*
North Carolina A&T University, 111
nullification, 62

Oakland, California, 82
Obama, Barack, 64, 147

Ohio, 64, 85. *See also* Cleveland, Ohio
Ohio State University, 20–21, 25, 97, 135, 137
Olympic Games, 139–141
Orthodox Judaism, 18–19, 26
out-of-state scholarship programs, 97
overcrowding, 89
Owens, Jesse, 140

Palestinian conflict, 147
Parks, Rosa, 106, 110
Park Synagogue, 18
Pasadena, California, 88
patents, 44
performative justice, 149
Philadelphia, Pennsylvania, 27, 78, 118
physical stereotypes, 12, 132, 154–155, 155–157
pig laws, 56
Pittsburgh Courier, 95
Plantation, The (neighborhood), 46
Plantation Room (at LSU), 46
plantations: and Black diet, 124; and Blacks' transition to freedom, 48–50, 53; glorification of, 45–47; and Hamer's background, 117–118; and origins of Jim Crow, 55–58; and sharecropping, 65–68; and Southern society, 47–48; and tourism in the South, 56–57
Plessy v. Ferguson, 100
police misconduct and violence: and author's class curricula, 1–2, 23–24, 28; author's personal experience with, 33–38; and Black Panther Party, 128; and police from the Deep South, 87; and protests of 2020, 29–30; and racial injustice dialogue, 152; and reform efforts, 143–144; and stereotyping, 154–155; and systemic racism, 32

political activism, 141-147. *See also* civil rights movement
political correctness/incorrectness, 4, 23
poll taxes, 62
Portland, Oregon, 82
poverty, 159
Prairie View A&M University, 97
predominantly white institutions (PWIs), 131, 135
prejudice, 52. *See also* racism; stereotypes
presidents, 51
pride in Blackness, 15
prisons, 67-68
private schools, 101
professional organizations, 73
"projects" (public housing), 89
property values, 92-93
protests of 2020, 29
Pruitt-Igoe, 89
public housing, 89, 145
public transportation, 92, 106-108, 145. *See also* Montgomery Bus Boycott
Pulaski, Tennessee, 58
push and pull factors, 77-78

Race in the Age of Obama (course), 36
Race in the Age of Trump (course), 158
race riots, 120-121
racism: and blockbusting, 92-93; and disenfranchisement of Blacks, 62-65; expressed in white student essays, 10-12, 12-14; fear of acknowledging, 32; racial fictions, 40; racial monopoly on power, 30-32; racial narratives, 40; racial steering, 88-89; racial stereotypes, 84; and recent immigrants to US, 25; and sexual anxieties, 103; and white allies, 158-160; of white parents, 24. *See also* police misconduct and violence
railroads, 30
Reconstruction, 57
redlining, 91-92
refinancing, 94
relationship building, 118
religion: and author's class curricula, 159; and informal codes of Jim Crow, 60; and legacy of plantation system, 53-54; and migration of Black Southerners, 80-81; and the Nation of Islam, 122-125; and student feedback in Black History classes, 11-12. *See also* churches
reparations, 7, 147
Republican Party, 64
required readings, 5
residency laws, 63
restrictive covenants, 92
reverse racism, 131-132
Robert Taylor Homes, 89
Rockwall County, Texas, 34
Roots (television series), 39, 43
runaway slaves, 43, 48-49
Russia, 110
Rust Belt, 86

salaries, 150
San Francisco, California, 82
Scholastic Aptitude Test (SAT), 137
school busing, 147
school curricula, 72
school overcrowding, 85
school segregation, 84-85, 97-102, 102-106
Schwerner, James, 118
Seale, Bobby, 128
Seattle, Washington, 82-83
secession, 75
Second Amendment, 106
Second Great Migration, 82
"seeing color," 151-152
segregation: and author's class

curricula, 10-11, 160; and Black institution building, 72-74; and Blacks outside the South, 120; and Black student organizations, 133; civil rights mobilizers vs. organizers, 109-111; and civil rights organizations, 113; and controversies surrounding Black history, 26; and key civil rights organizations, 113-119; and King's background, 127; and legacy of Civil War, 51-52; and military service of Blacks, 96; public transportation segregation, 106-108; and recent immigrants to US, 25; school segregation, 84-85, 97-102, 102-106; and sit-in movement, 111-112; and taxation, 65. *See also* Jim Crow
self-defense, 105-106
Selma, Alabama, 119
separate-but-equal doctrine, 98. *See also* segregation
separatists, 146, 147
sexual anxieties, 103
sexual assault, 34
Shakur, Afeni, 130-131
Shakur, Assata, 130
shame associated with Blackness, 10
sharecropping, 63, 65-67, 77-78, 81-82
Sharpton, Al, 112
Sherman, William Tecumseh, 51-52
sit-in movement, 111-112
slavery: as cause of Civil War, 75; causes and justifications for, 40-41; intergenerational effects of, 44-45; legacy of, 24-25; and Nation of Islam doctrine, 123; relationship to racism, 40-47; runaway slaves, 43, 48-49; and terminology issues, 39
Smart, Shaka, 154
Smith, Tommie, 141

socialism, 128
social order, 61
social programs, 159
social structure of the South, 47-48
soul food, 124
Souls to the Polls, 64
South Carolina, 43, 51, 52, 57, 96. *See also specific cities*
Southern Christian Leadership Council (SCLC), 113-115, 121
Southern states, 21-25, 101
Southern Whites, 47, 101
sports: and author's class curricula, 13; and author's speaking career, 161; Black power and college sports, 137-141; and stereotypes, 132, 154-155, 155-157
standardized testing, 8, 99, 136, 153
state constitutions, 62
states' rights, 62, 75
stereotypes: and author's class curricula, 10; author's experiences with, 154-155; and Black athletes, 132, 154-155, 155-157; and fraternities, 9; and micro-aggressions, 155-157; and racial Monopoly, 31-32
sterilization of Black women, 117
St. James Cemetery, 59
St. Louis, Missouri, 78, 142
St. Louis County, 1
Stokes, Carl, 143
Student Nonviolent Coordinating Committee (SNCC), 113-114, 117-118, 121
suburbs and suburbanization, 90, 91-92, 145
Sugar Land, Texas, 67
Summer Olympics (Mexico City, 1968), 139-141
Sun Belt, 86
Sundays, 60
Sweatt, Heman, 98-99
Sweatt v. Painter, 98-99
systemic racism, 32-33

Tallahatchie County, Mississippi, 117

taxation, 64-65, 136, 145-146

Taylor, Breonna, 28, 104

teaching assistants, 10

tenant farmers, 77-78. *See also* sharecropping

Tennessee, 43, 110. *See also specific cities*

terminology of race, 39

terrorism, 74

Texas: and admissions policies, 8; and American slave system, 43; and antigovernment sentiment, 101, 102; and anti-Muslim sentiment, 151; controversies surrounding Black history, 26-27; and disenfranchisement of Blacks, 65; and emancipation of slaves, 49; white primaries, 63. *See also specific cities*

Texas Southern University, 98

Texas State Capitol, 105-106

Texas State University for Negroes Law School, 98

textiles, 44. *See also* cotton cultivation

Thirteenth Amendment, 54, 56, 57-58, 62

"three-fifths compromise," 42

Till, Emmett, 61, 104-105

Till, Mamie, 104

Top 10 Percent Law, 8, 22

tourism, 45-46

trade skills, 41

traffic stops, 35-38

train travel, 80

"tricknology," 122

"triggering," 160

Trump, Donald, 24

Tulsa Race Riot, 74

unconscious bias, 152-154

undocumented workers, 151

Union Army, 48-49, 51

United Daughters of the Confederacy, 74-75

United States Olympic Committee (USOC), 139, 141

University of Alabama, 137

University of California, Berkeley, 97

University of California, Los Angeles, 34, 97, 141

University of California system, 148

University of Michigan, 97

University of Oklahoma, 155

University of Southern California, 137

University of Texas: and admissions process, 136-137; and author's teaching career, xv, 3, 21-22, 161; and Black student athletes, 137-139; and diversity initiatives, 149; and police misconduct, 34; and school desegregation campaign, 97-99; stereotypes and microaggressions at, 155-156; student feedback in Black History classes, 10-12, 12-14

University of Texas Law School, 98-99

University of Washington, 139

University Teaching Center (University of Texas), 2

Upper South, 43, 44

urbanization: and class divisions among Blacks, 83-84; and housing discrimination, 88-94; and job discrimination, 85-87; and migration of Black Southerners, 77-81, 81-83; and police brutality, 87; and public schooling, 84-85; and urban decline, 143; white resistance to Black migration, 81-83

US Army Corps of Engineers, 56

US Congress, 57

US Constitution, 42-43, 59, 95, 100, 128

US House of Representatives, 57
US Senate, 57
US Supreme Court, 85, 102-103, 114

vagrancy laws, 55-56
Veterans Administration (VA), 91
violence: assassinations, 52, 126-127, 131, 141, 146; associated with slavery, 45; against civil rights activists, 118; and disenfranchisement of Blacks, 63; and freedom rides, 114-115; and intimidation of Black voters, 103-104; and Montgomery Bus Boycott, 107; and police brutality, 87; and racial injustice dialogue, 148; white resistance to Black migration, 81-83. *See also* lynchings
Virginia, 43, 100
virtual lectures, xv, 29-30
voting rights: and civil rights activism outside the South, 121; and civil rights organizations, 113; and disenfranchisement of Blacks, 62-65; voter registration drives, 116-117, 142; Voting Rights Act of 1965, 32, 119; Voting Rights Act of 1968, 142; white resistance to Black voting, 103-104

Warmth of Other Suns, The (Wilkerson), 79-80
Washington, DC, 43
Washington, George, 42, 51
Washington Parish, Louisiana, 71-72
Watts riots, 120
welfare programs, 146

Wells, Ida B., 70
West Africa, 41
white allies, 158-160
White Citizens' Councils, 103-104
white flight, 90, 142
white fraternities, 9
white harmony narrative, 47-48
white newspapers, 120
white primaries, 63
white privilege, 11-12
white students, xiii-xiv, 3, 158
white supremacy ideology: and civil rights activism, 115-116; and disenfranchisement of Blacks, 63, 103; and freedom rides, 114-115; and lynching of Black veterans, 96; and Montgomery Bus Boycott, 112; and resistance to school desegregation, 99-100
Whitney, Eli, 44
Wilkerson, Isabel, 79-80
Williams, Mabel, 105
Williams, Robert F., 5, 105-106
Wilson, Darren, 1
Wilson, Jerome, xv, 71-72, 75
women activists, 109-111, 124-125
Women's Political Council, 106-108
Woodard, Isaac, 96
World War I, 77, 78
World War II, 77, 89-90, 95-96

X, Malcolm, 50-51, 111-112, 122, 125-127

yeoman farmers, 47-48
YouTube, 29-30

zip codes, 91-92
Zoom classes, 29-30

ABOUT THE AUTHOR

Leonard N. Moore is the George Littlefield Professor of American History at the University of Texas at Austin and a graduate of Jackson State University. He is the author of three books on Black politics, the most recent being *The Defeat of Black Power: Civil Rights and the National Black Political Convention of 1972.*